Table of Contents

The Law School Admission Test is a half-day standardized test required for admission to all ABA-approved law schools, most Canadian law schools, and many non-ABA-approved law schools. It consists of five 35-minute sections of multiple-choice questions. Four of the five sections contribute to the test taker's score. These sections include one reading comprehension section, one analytical reasoning section, and two logical reasoning sections. The unscored section, commonly referred to as the variable section, typically is used to pretest new test questions or to preequate new test forms. The placement of this section in the LSAT will vary. A 35-minute writing sample is administered at the end of the test. The writing sample is not scored by LSAC, but copies are sent to all law schools to which you apply. The score scale for the LSAT is 120 to 180.

The LSAT is designed to measure skills considered essential for success in law school: the reading and comprehension of complex texts with accuracy and insight; the organization and management of information and the ability to draw reasonable inferences from it; the ability to think critically; and the analysis and evaluation of the reasoning and arguments of others.

The LSAT provides a standard measure of acquired reading and verbal reasoning skills that law schools can use as one of several factors in assessing applicants.

For up-to-date information about LSAC's services, go to our website, *www.LSAC.org* or pick up a current *LSAC Information Book.*

Scoring

Your LSAT score is based on the number of questions you answer correctly (the raw score). There is no deduction for incorrect answers, and all questions count equally. In other words, there is no penalty for guessing.

■ Test Score Accuracy—Reliability and Standard Error of Measurement

Candidates perform at different levels on different occasions for reasons quite unrelated to the characteristics of a test itself. The accuracy of test scores is best described by the use of two related statistical terms: reliability and standard error of measurement.

Reliability is a measure of how consistently a test measures the skills being assessed. The higher the reliability coefficient for a test, the more certain we can be that test takers would get very similar scores if they took the test again.

LSAC reports an internal consistency measure of reliability for every test form. Reliability can vary from 0.00 to 1.00, and a test with no measurement error would have a reliability coefficient of 1.00 (never attained in practice). Reliability coefficients for past LSAT forms have ranged from .90 to .95, indicating a high degree of consistency for these tests. LSAC expects the reliability of the LSAT to continue to fall within the same range.

LSAC also reports the amount of measurement error associated with each test form, a concept known as the standard error of measurement (SEM). The SEM, which is usually about 2.6 points, indicates how close a test taker's observed score is likely to be to his or her true score. True scores are theoretical scores that would be obtained from perfectly reliable tests with no measurement error—scores never known in practice.

Score bands, or ranges of scores that contain a test taker's true score a certain percentage of the time, can be derived using the SEM. LSAT score bands are constructed by adding and subtracting the (rounded)

SEM to and from an actual LSAT score (e.g., the LSAT score, plus or minus 3 points). Scores near 120 or 180 have asymmetrical bands. Score bands constructed in this manner will contain an individual's true score approximately 68 percent of the time.

Measurement error also must be taken into account when comparing LSAT scores of two test takers. It is likely that small differences in scores are due to measurement error rather than to meaningful differences in ability. The standard error of score differences provides some guidance as to the importance of differences between two scores. The standard error of score differences is approximately 1.4 times larger than the standard error of measurement for the individual scores.

Thus, a test score should be regarded as a useful but approximate measure of a test taker's abilities as measured by the test, not as an exact determination of his or her abilities. LSAC encourages law schools to examine the range of scores within the interval that probably contains the test taker's true score (e.g., the test taker's score band) rather than solely interpret the reported score alone.

■ Adjustments for Variation in Test Difficulty

All test forms of the LSAT reported on the same score scale are designed to measure the same abilities, but one test form may be slightly easier or more difficult than another. The scores from different test forms are made comparable through a statistical procedure known as equating. As a result of equating, a given scaled score earned on different test forms reflects the same level of ability.

■ Research on the LSAT

Summaries of LSAT validity studies and other LSAT research can be found in member law school libraries.

■ To Inquire About Test Questions

If you find what you believe to be an error or ambiguity in a test question that affects your response to the question, contact LSAC by e-mail: *LSATTS@LSAC.org*, or write to Law School Admission Council, Test Development Group, Box 40, Newtown, PA 18940-0040.

How This PrepTest Differs From an Actual LSAT

This PrepTest is made up of the scored sections and writing sample from the actual disclosed LSAT administered in June 2009. However, it does not contain the extra, variable section that is used to pretest new test items of one of the three multiple-choice question types. The three multiple-choice question types may be in a different order in an actual LSAT than in this PrepTest. This is because the order of these question types is intentionally varied for each administration of the test.

The Question Types

The multiple-choice questions that make up most of the LSAT reflect a broad range of academic disciplines and are intended to give no advantage to candidates from a particular academic background.

The five sections of the test contain three different question types. The following material presents a general discussion of the nature of each question type and some strategies that can be used in answering them.

■ Analytical Reasoning Questions

Analytical reasoning items are designed to measure your ability to understand a structure of relationships and to draw logical conclusions about the structure. You are asked to make deductions from a set of statements, rules, or conditions that describe relationships among entities such as persons, places, things, or events. They simulate the kinds of detailed analyses of relationships that a law student must perform in solving legal problems. For example, a passage might describe four diplomats sitting around a table, following certain rules of protocol as to who can sit where. You must answer questions about the implications of the given information, for example, who is sitting between diplomats X and Y.

The passage used for each group of questions describes a common relationship such as the following:

- Assignment: Two parents, P and O, and their children, R and S, must go to the dentist on four consecutive days, designated 1, 2, 3, and 4;

- Ordering: X arrived before Y but after Z;

- Grouping: A manager is trying to form a project team from seven staff members—R, S, T, U, V, W, and X. Each staff member has a particular strength—writing, planning, or facilitating;

- Spatial: A certain country contains six cities and each city is connected to at least one other city by a system of roads, some of which are one-way.

Careful reading and analysis are necessary to determine the exact nature of the relationships involved. Some relationships are fixed (e.g., P and R always sit at the same table). Other relationships are variable (e.g., Q must be assigned to either table 1 or table 3). Some relationships that are not stated in the conditions are implied by and can be deduced from those that are stated. (e.g., If one condition about books on a shelf specifies that Book L is to the left of Book Y, and another specifies that Book P is to the left of Book L, then it can be deduced that Book P is to the left of Book Y.)

No formal training in logic is required to answer these questions correctly. Analytical reasoning questions are intended to be answered using knowledge, skills, and reasoning ability generally expected of college students and graduates.

Suggested Approach

Some people may prefer to answer first those questions about a passage that seem less difficult and then those that seem more difficult. In general, it is best not to start another passage before finishing one begun earlier, because much time can be lost in returning to a passage and reestablishing familiarity with its relationships. Do not assume that, because the conditions for a set of questions look long or complicated, the questions based on those conditions will necessarily be especially difficult.

Reading the passage. In reading the conditions, do not introduce unwarranted assumptions. For instance, in a set establishing relationships of height and weight among the members of a team, do not assume that a person who is taller than another person must weigh more than that person. All the information needed to answer each question is provided in the passage and the question itself.

The conditions are designed to be as clear as possible; do not interpret them as if they were intended to trick you. For example, if a question asks how many people could be eligible to serve on a committee, consider only those people named in the passage unless directed otherwise. When in doubt, read the conditions in their most obvious sense. Remember, however, that the language in the conditions is intended to be read for precise meaning. It is essential to pay particular attention to words that describe or limit relationships, such as "only," "exactly," "never," "always," "must be," "cannot be," and the like.

The result of this careful reading will be a clear picture of the structure of the relationships involved, including the kinds of relationships permitted, the participants in the relationships, and the range of actions or attributes allowed by the relationships for these participants.

Questions are independent. Each question should be considered separately from the other questions in its set; no information, except what is given in the original conditions, should be carried over from one question to another. In some cases a question will simply ask for conclusions to be drawn from the conditions as originally given. Some questions may, however, add information to the original conditions or temporarily suspend one of the original conditions for the purpose of that question only. For example, if Question 1 adds the information "if P is sitting at table 2 ...," this information should NOT be carried over to any other question in the group.

Highlighting the text; using diagrams. Many people find it useful to underline key points in the passage and in each question. In addition, it may prove very helpful to draw a diagram to assist you in finding the solution to the problem.

In preparing for the test, you may wish to experiment with different types of diagrams. For a scheduling problem, a calendar-like diagram may be helpful. For a spatial relationship problem, a simple map can be a useful device.

Even though some people find diagrams to be very helpful, other people seldom use them. And among those who do regularly use diagrams in solving these problems, there is by no means universal agreement on which kind of diagram is best for which problem or in which cases a diagram is most useful. Do not be concerned if a particular problem in the test seems to be best approached without the use of a diagram.

■ Logical Reasoning Questions

Logical reasoning questions evaluate your ability to understand, analyze, criticize, and complete a variety of arguments. The arguments are contained in short passages taken from a variety of sources, including letters to the editor, speeches, advertisements, newspaper articles and editorials, informal discussions and conversations, as well as articles in the humanities, the social sciences, and the natural sciences.

Each logical reasoning question requires you to read and comprehend a short passage, then answer one or two questions about it. The questions test a variety of abilities involved in reasoning logically and thinking critically. These include:

- recognizing the point or issue of an argument or dispute;

- detecting the assumptions involved in an argumentation or chain of reasoning;

- drawing reasonable conclusions from given evidence or premises;

- identifying and applying principles;

- identifying the method or structure of an argument or chain of reasoning;

- detecting reasoning errors and misinterpretations;

- determining how additional evidence or argumentation affects an argument or conclusion; and

- identifying explanations and recognizing resolutions of conflicting facts or arguments.

The questions do not presuppose knowledge of the terminology of formal logic. For example, you will not be expected to know the meaning of specialized terms such as "ad hominem" or "syllogism." On the other hand, you will be expected to understand and critique the reasoning contained in arguments. This requires that you possess, at a minimum, a college-level understanding of widely used concepts such as argument, premise, assumption, and conclusion.

Suggested Approach

Read each question carefully. Make sure that you understand the meaning of each part of the question. Make sure that you understand the meaning of each answer choice and the ways in which it may or may not relate to the question posed.

Do not pick a response simply because it is a true statement. Although true, it may not answer the question posed.

Answer each question on the basis of the information that is given, even if you do not agree with it. Work within the context provided by the passage. LSAT questions do not involve any tricks or hidden meanings.

■ Reading Comprehension Questions

The purpose of reading comprehension questions is to measure your ability to read, with understanding and insight, examples of lengthy and complex materials similar to those commonly encountered in law school work. The reading comprehension section of the LSAT contains four sets of reading questions, each consisting of a selection of reading material followed by five to eight questions. The reading selection in three of the four sets consists of a single reading passage of approximately 450 words in length. The other set contains two related shorter passages. Sets with two passages are a new variant of reading comprehension, called comparative reading, which were introduced into the reading comprehension section in June 2007. See "Comparative Reading" below for more information.

Reading selections for reading comprehension questions are drawn from subjects such as the humanities, the social sciences, the biological and physical sciences, and issues related to the law. Reading comprehension questions require you to read carefully and accurately, to determine the relationships among the various parts of the reading selection, and to draw reasonable inferences from the material in the selection. The questions may ask about the following characteristics of a passage or pair of passages:

- the main idea or primary purpose;
- the meaning or purpose of words or phrases used;
- information explicitly stated;
- information or ideas that can be inferred;
- the organization or structure;
- the application of information in a passage to a new context; and
- the author's attitude as it is revealed in the tone of a passage or the language used.

Suggested Approach

Since reading selections are drawn from many different disciplines and sources, you should not be discouraged if you encounter material with which you are not familiar. It is important to remember that questions are to be answered exclusively on the basis of the information provided in the selection. There is no particular knowledge that you are expected to bring to the test, and you should not make inferences based on any prior knowledge of a subject that you may have. You may, however, wish to defer working on a set of questions that seems particularly difficult or unfamiliar until after you have dealt with sets you find easier.

Strategies. In preparing for the test, you should experiment with different strategies and decide which work most effectively for you. These include:

- reading the selection very closely and then answering the questions;
- reading the questions first, reading the selection closely, and then returning to the questions; or
- skimming the selection and questions very quickly, then rereading the selection closely and answering the questions.

Remember that your strategy must be effective for you under timed conditions.

Reading the selection. Whatever strategy you choose, you should give the passage or pair of passages at least one careful reading before answering the questions. Try to distinguish main ideas from supporting ideas, and opinions or attitudes from factual, objective information. Note transitions from one idea to the next and examine the relationships among the different ideas or parts of a passage, or between the two passages in comparative reading sets. Consider how and why an author makes points and draws conclusions. Be sensitive to implications of what the passages say.

You may find it helpful to mark key parts of passages. For example, you might underline main ideas or important arguments, and you might circle transitional words—"although," "nevertheless," "correspondingly," and the like—that will help you map the structure of a passage. Moreover, you might note descriptive words that will help you identify an author's attitude toward a particular idea or person.

Answering the Questions

- Always read all the answer choices before selecting the best answer. The best answer choice is the one that most accurately and completely answers the question being posed.

- Respond to the specific question being asked. Do not pick an answer choice simply because it is a true statement. For example, picking a true statement might yield an incorrect answer to a question in which you are asked to identify an author's position on an issue, since here you are not being asked to evaluate the truth of the author's position but only to correctly identify what that position is.

- Answer the questions only on the basis of the information provided in the selection. Your own views, interpretations, or opinions, and those you have heard from others, may sometimes conflict with those expressed in a reading selection; however, you are expected to work within the context provided by the reading selection. You should not expect to agree with everything you encounter in reading comprehension passages.

■ Comparative Reading

As of the June 2007 administration, LSAC introduced a new variant of reading comprehension, called comparative reading, as one of the four sets in the LSAT reading comprehension section. In general, comparative reading questions are similar to traditional reading comprehension questions, except that comparative reading questions are based on two shorter passages instead of one longer passage. The two passages together are of roughly the same length as one reading comprehension passage, so the total amount of reading in the reading comprehension section remains essentially the same. A few of the questions that follow a comparative reading passage pair might concern only one of the two passages, but most will be about both passages and how they relate to each other.

Comparative reading questions reflect the nature of some important tasks in law school work, such as understanding arguments from multiple texts by applying skills of comparison, contrast, generalization, and synthesis to the texts. The purpose of comparative reading is to assess this important set of skills directly.

What Comparative Reading Looks Like

The two passages in a comparative reading set—labeled **"Passage A"** and **"Passage B"**—discuss the same topic or related topics. The topics fall into the same academic categories traditionally used in reading comprehension: humanities, natural sciences, social sciences, and issues related to the law. Like traditional reading comprehension passages, comparative reading passages are complex and generally involve argument. The two passages in a comparative reading pair are typically adapted from two different published sources written by two different authors. They are usually independent of each other, with neither author responding directly to the other.

As you read the pair of passages, it is helpful to try to determine what the central idea or main point of each passage is, and to determine how the passages relate to each other. The passages will relate to each other in various ways. In some cases, the authors of the passages will be in general agreement with each other, while in others their views will be directly opposed. Passage pairs may also exhibit more complex types of relationships: for example, one passage might articulate a set of principles, while the other passage applies those or similar principles to a particular situation.

Questions that are concerned with only one of the passages are essentially identical to traditional reading comprehension questions. Questions that address both passages test the same fundamental reading skills as traditional reading comprehension questions, but the skills are applied to two texts instead of one. You may be asked to identify a main purpose shared by both passages, a statement with which both authors would agree, or a similarity or dissimilarity in the structure of the arguments in the two passages. The following are additional examples of comparative reading questions:

- Which one of the following is the central topic of each passage?

- Both passages explicitly mention which one of the following?

- Which one of the following statements is most strongly supported by both passages?

- Which one of the following most accurately describes the attitude expressed by the author of passage B toward the overall argument in passage A?

- The relationship between passage A and passage B is most analogous to the relationship in which one of the following?

This is not a complete list of the sorts of questions you may be asked in a comparative reading set, but it illustrates the range of questions you may be asked.

The Writing Sample

On the day of the test, you will be asked to write one sample essay. LSAC does not score the writing sample, but copies are sent to all law schools to which you apply. According to a 2006 LSAC survey of 157 United States and Canadian law schools, almost all utilize the writing sample in evaluating some applications for admission. Frivolous responses or no responses to writing sample prompts have been used by law schools as grounds for rejection of applications for admission.

In developing and implementing the writing sample portion of the LSAT, LSAC has operated on the following premises: First, law schools and the legal profession value highly the ability to communicate effectively in writing. Second, it is important to encourage potential law students to develop effective writing skills. Third, a sample of an applicant's writing, produced under controlled conditions, is a potentially useful indication of that

person's writing ability. Fourth, the writing sample can serve as an independent check on other writing submitted by applicants as part of the admission process. Finally, writing samples may be useful for diagnostic purposes.

You will have 35 minutes in which to plan and write an essay on the topic you receive. Read the topic and the accompanying directions carefully. You will probably find it best to spend a few minutes considering the topic and organizing your thoughts before you begin writing. In your essay, be sure to develop your ideas fully, leaving time, if possible, to review what you have written. Do not write on a topic other than the one specified. Writing on a topic of your own choice is not acceptable.

No special knowledge is required or expected for this writing exercise. Law schools are interested in the reasoning, clarity, organization, language usage, and writing mechanics displayed in your essay. How well you write is more important than how much you write. Confine your essay to the blocked, lined area on the front and back of the Writing Sample Response Sheet. Only that area will be reproduced for law schools. Be sure that your writing is legible.

The writing prompt presents a decision problem. You are asked to make a choice between two positions or courses of action. Both of the choices are defensible, and you are given criteria and facts on which to base your decision. There is no "right" or "wrong" position to take on the topic, so the quality of each test taker's response is a function not of which choice is made, but of how well or poorly the choice is supported and how well or poorly the other choice is criticized.

Taking the PrepTest Under Simulated LSAT Conditions

One important way to prepare for the LSAT is to simulate the day of the test by taking a practice test under actual time constraints. Taking a practice test under timed conditions helps you to estimate the amount of time you can afford to spend on each question in a section and to determine the question types on which you may need additional practice.

Since the LSAT is a timed test, it is important to use your allotted time wisely. During the test, you may work only on the section designated by the test supervisor. You cannot devote extra time to a difficult section and make up that time on a section you find easier. In pacing yourself, and checking your answers, you should think of each section of the test as a separate minitest.

Be sure that you answer every question on the test. When you do not know the correct answer to a question, first eliminate the responses that you know are incorrect, then make your best guess among the remaining choices. Do not be afraid to guess as there is no penalty for incorrect answers.

When you take a practice test, abide by all the requirements specified in the directions and keep strictly within the specified time limits. Work without a rest period. When you take an actual test, you will have only a short break—usually 10-15 minutes—after SECTION III. When taken under conditions as much like actual testing conditions as possible, a practice test provides very useful preparation for taking the LSAT.

Official directions for the four multiple-choice sections and the writing sample are included in this PrepTest so that you can approximate actual testing conditions as you practice.

To take the test:

- Set a timer for 35 minutes. Answer all the questions in SECTION I of this PrepTest. Stop working on that section when the 35 minutes have elapsed.

- Repeat, allowing yourself 35 minutes each for sections II, III, and IV.

- Set the timer again for 35 minutes, then prepare your response to the writing sample topic at the end of this PrepTest.

- Refer to "Computing Your Score" for the PrepTest for instruction on evaluating your performance. An answer key is provided for that purpose.

The practice test that follows consists of four sections corresponding to the four scored sections of the June 2009 LSAT. Also reprinted is the June 2009 unscored writing sample topic.

General Directions for the LSAT Answer Sheet

The actual testing time for this portion of the test will be 2 hours 55 minutes. There are five sections, each with a time limit of 35 minutes. The supervisor will tell you when to begin and end each section. If you finish a section before time is called, you may check your work on that section <u>only</u>; do not turn to any other section of the test book and do not work on any other section either in the test book or on the answer sheet.

There are several different types of questions on the test, and each question type has its own directions. <u>Be sure you understand the directions for each question type before attempting to answer any questions in that section.</u>

Not everyone will finish all the questions in the time allowed. Do not hurry, but work steadily and as quickly as you can without sacrificing accuracy. You are advised to use your time effectively. If a question seems too difficult, go on to the next one and return to the difficult question after completing the section. MARK THE BEST ANSWER YOU CAN FOR EVERY QUESTION. NO DEDUCTIONS WILL BE MADE FOR WRONG ANSWERS. YOUR SCORE WILL BE BASED ONLY ON THE NUMBER OF QUESTIONS YOU ANSWER CORRECTLY.

ALL YOUR ANSWERS MUST BE MARKED ON THE ANSWER SHEET. Answer spaces for each question are lettered to correspond with the letters of the potential answers to each question in the test book. After you have decided which of the answers is correct, blacken the corresponding space on the answer sheet. BE SURE THAT EACH MARK IS BLACK AND COMPLETELY FILLS THE ANSWER SPACE. Give only one answer to each question. If you change an answer, be sure that all previous marks are <u>erased completely</u>. Since the answer sheet is machine scored, incomplete erasures may be interpreted as intended answers. ANSWERS RECORDED IN THE TEST BOOK WILL NOT BE SCORED.

There may be more questions noted on this answer sheet than there are questions in a section. Do not be concerned but be certain that the section and number of the question you are answering matches the answer sheet section and question number. Additional answer spaces in any answer sheet section should be left blank. Begin your next section in the number one answer space for that section.

LSAC takes various steps to ensure that answer sheets are returned from test centers in a timely manner for processing. In the unlikely event that an answer sheet(s) is not received, LSAC will permit the examinee to either retest at no additional fee or to receive a refund of his or her LSAT fee. THESE REMEDIES ARE THE EXCLUSIVE REMEDIES AVAILABLE IN THE UNLIKELY EVENT THAT AN ANSWER SHEET IS NOT RECEIVED BY LSAC.

Score Cancellation

Complete this section only if you are absolutely certain you want to cancel your score. A CANCELLATION RE-QUEST CANNOT BE RESCINDED. IF YOU ARE AT ALL UNCERTAIN, YOU SHOULD <u>NOT</u> COMPLETE THIS SECTION.

To cancel your score from this administration, you **must:**

A. fill in both ovals here ..... ○ ○
   AND
B. read the following statement. Then sign your name and enter the date.
   YOUR SIGNATURE ALONE IS NOT SUFFICIENT FOR SCORE CANCELLATION. BOTH OVALS ABOVE MUST BE FILLED IN FOR SCANNING EQUIPMENT TO RECOGNIZE YOUR REQUEST FOR SCORE CANCELLATION.

I certify that I wish to cancel my test score from this administration. I understand that my request is irreversible and that my score will not be sent to me or to the law schools to which I apply.

_____
Sign your name in full

_____
Date

FOR LSAC USE ONLY ⬤

HOW DID YOU PREPARE FOR THE LSAT?
(Select all that apply.)

Responses to this item are voluntary and will be used for statistical research purposes only.

- ○ By studying the sample questions in the *LSAT & LSDAS Information Book.*
- ○ By taking the free sample LSAT in the *LSAT & LSDAS Information Book.*
- ○ By working through official LSAT *PrepTests, ItemWise,* and/or other LSAC test prep products.
- ○ By using LSAT prep books or software not published by LSAC.
- ○ By attending a commercial test preparation or coaching course.
- ○ By attending a test preparation or coaching course offered through an undergraduate institution.
- ○ Self study.
- ○ Other preparation.
- ○ No preparation.

CERTIFYING STATEMENT

Please write (DO NOT PRINT) the following statement. Sign and date.

I certify that I am the examinee whose name appears on this answer sheet and that I am here to take the LSAT for the sole purpose of being considered for admission to law school. I further certify that I will neither assist nor receive assistance from any other candidate, and I agree not to copy or retain examination questions or to transmit them to or discuss them with any other person in any form.

_____
_____
_____
_____
_____
_____
_____
_____
_____

SIGNATURE: _____ TODAY'S DATE: ___/___/___
                                                              MONTH DAY YEAR

SCANTRON® EliteView™ EM-250133-8:654321

USE A NO. 2 OR HB PENCIL ONLY

● Right Mark   ⊘ ⊗ ⊙ Wrong Marks

A

1 LAST NAME / FIRST NAME / MI

2 SOCIAL SECURITY/ SOCIAL INSURANCE NO.

3 LSAC ACCOUNT NUMBER

L

4 DATE OF BIRTH

MONTH	DAY	YEAR
○ Jan		
○ Feb		
○ Mar		
○ Apr		
○ May		
○ June		
○ July		
○ Aug		
○ Sept		
○ Oct		
○ Nov		
○ Dec		

5 RACIAL/ETHNIC DESCRIPTION

Mark one or more

○ 1 Aboriginal/TSI Australian
○ 2 Amer. Indian/Alaska Native
○ 3 Asian
○ 4 Black/African American
○ 5 Canadian Aboriginal
○ 6 Caucasian/White
○ 7 Hispanic/Latino
○ 8 Native Hawaiian/Other Pacific Islander
○ 9 Puerto Rican

6 GENDER
○ Male
○ Female

7 DOMINANT LANGUAGE
○ English
○ Other

8 ENGLISH FLUENCY
○ Yes   ○ No

9 TEST BOOK SERIAL NO.

10 TEST FORM

11 TEST DATE

MONTH   DAY   YEAR

12 CENTER NUMBER

13 TEST FORM CODE

Law School Admission Test

Mark one and only one answer to each question. Be sure to fill in completely the space for your intended answer choice. If you erase, do so completely. Make no stray marks.

SECTION 1	SECTION 2	SECTION 3	SECTION 4	SECTION 5
1 Ⓐ Ⓑ Ⓒ Ⓓ Ⓔ	1 Ⓐ Ⓑ Ⓒ Ⓓ Ⓔ	1 Ⓐ Ⓑ Ⓒ Ⓓ Ⓔ	1 Ⓐ Ⓑ Ⓒ Ⓓ Ⓔ	1 Ⓐ Ⓑ Ⓒ Ⓓ Ⓔ
2 Ⓐ Ⓑ Ⓒ Ⓓ Ⓔ	2 Ⓐ Ⓑ Ⓒ Ⓓ Ⓔ	2 Ⓐ Ⓑ Ⓒ Ⓓ Ⓔ	2 Ⓐ Ⓑ Ⓒ Ⓓ Ⓔ	2 Ⓐ Ⓑ Ⓒ Ⓓ Ⓔ
3 Ⓐ Ⓑ Ⓒ Ⓓ Ⓔ	3 Ⓐ Ⓑ Ⓒ Ⓓ Ⓔ	3 Ⓐ Ⓑ Ⓒ Ⓓ Ⓔ	3 Ⓐ Ⓑ Ⓒ Ⓓ Ⓔ	3 Ⓐ Ⓑ Ⓒ Ⓓ Ⓔ
4 Ⓐ Ⓑ Ⓒ Ⓓ Ⓔ	4 Ⓐ Ⓑ Ⓒ Ⓓ Ⓔ	4 Ⓐ Ⓑ Ⓒ Ⓓ Ⓔ	4 Ⓐ Ⓑ Ⓒ Ⓓ Ⓔ	4 Ⓐ Ⓑ Ⓒ Ⓓ Ⓔ
5 Ⓐ Ⓑ Ⓒ Ⓓ Ⓔ	5 Ⓐ Ⓑ Ⓒ Ⓓ Ⓔ	5 Ⓐ Ⓑ Ⓒ Ⓓ Ⓔ	5 Ⓐ Ⓑ Ⓒ Ⓓ Ⓔ	5 Ⓐ Ⓑ Ⓒ Ⓓ Ⓔ
6 Ⓐ Ⓑ Ⓒ Ⓓ Ⓔ	6 Ⓐ Ⓑ Ⓒ Ⓓ Ⓔ	6 Ⓐ Ⓑ Ⓒ Ⓓ Ⓔ	6 Ⓐ Ⓑ Ⓒ Ⓓ Ⓔ	6 Ⓐ Ⓑ Ⓒ Ⓓ Ⓔ
7 Ⓐ Ⓑ Ⓒ Ⓓ Ⓔ	7 Ⓐ Ⓑ Ⓒ Ⓓ Ⓔ	7 Ⓐ Ⓑ Ⓒ Ⓓ Ⓔ	7 Ⓐ Ⓑ Ⓒ Ⓓ Ⓔ	7 Ⓐ Ⓑ Ⓒ Ⓓ Ⓔ
8 Ⓐ Ⓑ Ⓒ Ⓓ Ⓔ	8 Ⓐ Ⓑ Ⓒ Ⓓ Ⓔ	8 Ⓐ Ⓑ Ⓒ Ⓓ Ⓔ	8 Ⓐ Ⓑ Ⓒ Ⓓ Ⓔ	8 Ⓐ Ⓑ Ⓒ Ⓓ Ⓔ
9 Ⓐ Ⓑ Ⓒ Ⓓ Ⓔ	9 Ⓐ Ⓑ Ⓒ Ⓓ Ⓔ	9 Ⓐ Ⓑ Ⓒ Ⓓ Ⓔ	9 Ⓐ Ⓑ Ⓒ Ⓓ Ⓔ	9 Ⓐ Ⓑ Ⓒ Ⓓ Ⓔ
10 Ⓐ Ⓑ Ⓒ Ⓓ Ⓔ	10 Ⓐ Ⓑ Ⓒ Ⓓ Ⓔ	10 Ⓐ Ⓑ Ⓒ Ⓓ Ⓔ	10 Ⓐ Ⓑ Ⓒ Ⓓ Ⓔ	10 Ⓐ Ⓑ Ⓒ Ⓓ Ⓔ
11 Ⓐ Ⓑ Ⓒ Ⓓ Ⓔ	11 Ⓐ Ⓑ Ⓒ Ⓓ Ⓔ	11 Ⓐ Ⓑ Ⓒ Ⓓ Ⓔ	11 Ⓐ Ⓑ Ⓒ Ⓓ Ⓔ	11 Ⓐ Ⓑ Ⓒ Ⓓ Ⓔ
12 Ⓐ Ⓑ Ⓒ Ⓓ Ⓔ	12 Ⓐ Ⓑ Ⓒ Ⓓ Ⓔ	12 Ⓐ Ⓑ Ⓒ Ⓓ Ⓔ	12 Ⓐ Ⓑ Ⓒ Ⓓ Ⓔ	12 Ⓐ Ⓑ Ⓒ Ⓓ Ⓔ
13 Ⓐ Ⓑ Ⓒ Ⓓ Ⓔ	13 Ⓐ Ⓑ Ⓒ Ⓓ Ⓔ	13 Ⓐ Ⓑ Ⓒ Ⓓ Ⓔ	13 Ⓐ Ⓑ Ⓒ Ⓓ Ⓔ	13 Ⓐ Ⓑ Ⓒ Ⓓ Ⓔ
14 Ⓐ Ⓑ Ⓒ Ⓓ Ⓔ	14 Ⓐ Ⓑ Ⓒ Ⓓ Ⓔ	14 Ⓐ Ⓑ Ⓒ Ⓓ Ⓔ	14 Ⓐ Ⓑ Ⓒ Ⓓ Ⓔ	14 Ⓐ Ⓑ Ⓒ Ⓓ Ⓔ
15 Ⓐ Ⓑ Ⓒ Ⓓ Ⓔ	15 Ⓐ Ⓑ Ⓒ Ⓓ Ⓔ	15 Ⓐ Ⓑ Ⓒ Ⓓ Ⓔ	15 Ⓐ Ⓑ Ⓒ Ⓓ Ⓔ	15 Ⓐ Ⓑ Ⓒ Ⓓ Ⓔ
16 Ⓐ Ⓑ Ⓒ Ⓓ Ⓔ	16 Ⓐ Ⓑ Ⓒ Ⓓ Ⓔ	16 Ⓐ Ⓑ Ⓒ Ⓓ Ⓔ	16 Ⓐ Ⓑ Ⓒ Ⓓ Ⓔ	16 Ⓐ Ⓑ Ⓒ Ⓓ Ⓔ
17 Ⓐ Ⓑ Ⓒ Ⓓ Ⓔ	17 Ⓐ Ⓑ Ⓒ Ⓓ Ⓔ	17 Ⓐ Ⓑ Ⓒ Ⓓ Ⓔ	17 Ⓐ Ⓑ Ⓒ Ⓓ Ⓔ	17 Ⓐ Ⓑ Ⓒ Ⓓ Ⓔ
18 Ⓐ Ⓑ Ⓒ Ⓓ Ⓔ	18 Ⓐ Ⓑ Ⓒ Ⓓ Ⓔ	18 Ⓐ Ⓑ Ⓒ Ⓓ Ⓔ	18 Ⓐ Ⓑ Ⓒ Ⓓ Ⓔ	18 Ⓐ Ⓑ Ⓒ Ⓓ Ⓔ
19 Ⓐ Ⓑ Ⓒ Ⓓ Ⓔ	19 Ⓐ Ⓑ Ⓒ Ⓓ Ⓔ	19 Ⓐ Ⓑ Ⓒ Ⓓ Ⓔ	19 Ⓐ Ⓑ Ⓒ Ⓓ Ⓔ	19 Ⓐ Ⓑ Ⓒ Ⓓ Ⓔ
20 Ⓐ Ⓑ Ⓒ Ⓓ Ⓔ	20 Ⓐ Ⓑ Ⓒ Ⓓ Ⓔ	20 Ⓐ Ⓑ Ⓒ Ⓓ Ⓔ	20 Ⓐ Ⓑ Ⓒ Ⓓ Ⓔ	20 Ⓐ Ⓑ Ⓒ Ⓓ Ⓔ
21 Ⓐ Ⓑ Ⓒ Ⓓ Ⓔ	21 Ⓐ Ⓑ Ⓒ Ⓓ Ⓔ	21 Ⓐ Ⓑ Ⓒ Ⓓ Ⓔ	21 Ⓐ Ⓑ Ⓒ Ⓓ Ⓔ	21 Ⓐ Ⓑ Ⓒ Ⓓ Ⓔ
22 Ⓐ Ⓑ Ⓒ Ⓓ Ⓔ	22 Ⓐ Ⓑ Ⓒ Ⓓ Ⓔ	22 Ⓐ Ⓑ Ⓒ Ⓓ Ⓔ	22 Ⓐ Ⓑ Ⓒ Ⓓ Ⓔ	22 Ⓐ Ⓑ Ⓒ Ⓓ Ⓔ
23 Ⓐ Ⓑ Ⓒ Ⓓ Ⓔ	23 Ⓐ Ⓑ Ⓒ Ⓓ Ⓔ	23 Ⓐ Ⓑ Ⓒ Ⓓ Ⓔ	23 Ⓐ Ⓑ Ⓒ Ⓓ Ⓔ	23 Ⓐ Ⓑ Ⓒ Ⓓ Ⓔ
24 Ⓐ Ⓑ Ⓒ Ⓓ Ⓔ	24 Ⓐ Ⓑ Ⓒ Ⓓ Ⓔ	24 Ⓐ Ⓑ Ⓒ Ⓓ Ⓔ	24 Ⓐ Ⓑ Ⓒ Ⓓ Ⓔ	24 Ⓐ Ⓑ Ⓒ Ⓓ Ⓔ
25 Ⓐ Ⓑ Ⓒ Ⓓ Ⓔ	25 Ⓐ Ⓑ Ⓒ Ⓓ Ⓔ	25 Ⓐ Ⓑ Ⓒ Ⓓ Ⓔ	25 Ⓐ Ⓑ Ⓒ Ⓓ Ⓔ	25 Ⓐ Ⓑ Ⓒ Ⓓ Ⓔ
26 Ⓐ Ⓑ Ⓒ Ⓓ Ⓔ	26 Ⓐ Ⓑ Ⓒ Ⓓ Ⓔ	26 Ⓐ Ⓑ Ⓒ Ⓓ Ⓔ	26 Ⓐ Ⓑ Ⓒ Ⓓ Ⓔ	26 Ⓐ Ⓑ Ⓒ Ⓓ Ⓔ
27 Ⓐ Ⓑ Ⓒ Ⓓ Ⓔ	27 Ⓐ Ⓑ Ⓒ Ⓓ Ⓔ	27 Ⓐ Ⓑ Ⓒ Ⓓ Ⓔ	27 Ⓐ Ⓑ Ⓒ Ⓓ Ⓔ	27 Ⓐ Ⓑ Ⓒ Ⓓ Ⓔ
28 Ⓐ Ⓑ Ⓒ Ⓓ Ⓔ	28 Ⓐ Ⓑ Ⓒ Ⓓ Ⓔ	28 Ⓐ Ⓑ Ⓒ Ⓓ Ⓔ	28 Ⓐ Ⓑ Ⓒ Ⓓ Ⓔ	28 Ⓐ Ⓑ Ⓒ Ⓓ Ⓔ
29 Ⓐ Ⓑ Ⓒ Ⓓ Ⓔ	29 Ⓐ Ⓑ Ⓒ Ⓓ Ⓔ	29 Ⓐ Ⓑ Ⓒ Ⓓ Ⓔ	29 Ⓐ Ⓑ Ⓒ Ⓓ Ⓔ	29 Ⓐ Ⓑ Ⓒ Ⓓ Ⓔ
30 Ⓐ Ⓑ Ⓒ Ⓓ Ⓔ	30 Ⓐ Ⓑ Ⓒ Ⓓ Ⓔ	30 Ⓐ Ⓑ Ⓒ Ⓓ Ⓔ	30 Ⓐ Ⓑ Ⓒ Ⓓ Ⓔ	30 Ⓐ Ⓑ Ⓒ Ⓓ Ⓔ

14 PLEASE PRINT ALL INFORMATION

LAST NAME   FIRST

SOCIAL SECURITY/SOCIAL INSURANCE NO.

DATE OF BIRTH

MAILING ADDRESS

NOTE: If you have a new address, you must write LSAC at Box 2000-C, Newtown, PA 18940 or call 215.968.1001.

FOR LSAC USE ONLY		
LR	LW	LCS

● ⊖Ⓔ

SECTION I

Time—35 minutes

23 Questions

Directions: Each group of questions in this section is based on a set of conditions. In answering some of the questions, it may be useful to draw a rough diagram. Choose the response that most accurately and completely answers each question and blacken the corresponding space on your answer sheet.

Questions 1–5

On a particular Saturday, a student will perform six activities—grocery shopping, hedge trimming, jogging, kitchen cleaning, laundry, and motorbike servicing. Each activity will be performed once, one at a time. The order in which the activities are performed is subject to the following conditions:

Grocery shopping has to be immediately after hedge trimming.

Kitchen cleaning has to be earlier than grocery shopping.

Motorbike servicing has to be earlier than laundry.

Motorbike servicing has to be either immediately before or immediately after jogging.

1. Which one of the following could be the order, from first to last, of the student's activities?

   (A)   jogging, kitchen cleaning, hedge trimming, grocery shopping, motorbike servicing, laundry
   (B)   jogging, motorbike servicing, laundry, hedge trimming, grocery shopping, kitchen cleaning
   (C)   kitchen cleaning, hedge trimming, grocery shopping, laundry, motorbike servicing, jogging
   (D)   kitchen cleaning, jogging, motorbike servicing, laundry, hedge trimming, grocery shopping
   (E)   motorbike servicing, jogging, laundry, hedge trimming, kitchen cleaning, grocery shopping

2. Which one of the following activities CANNOT be third?

   (A)   grocery shopping
   (B)   hedge trimming
   (C)   jogging
   (D)   kitchen cleaning
   (E)   motorbike servicing

3. Which one of the following CANNOT be true?

   (A)   Hedge trimming is fourth.
   (B)   Jogging is fourth.
   (C)   Kitchen cleaning is second.
   (D)   Laundry is third.
   (E)   Motorbike servicing is second.

4. Which one of the following activities CANNOT be fifth?

   (A)   grocery shopping
   (B)   hedge trimming
   (C)   jogging
   (D)   laundry
   (E)   motorbike servicing

5. Which one of the following, if substituted for the condition that motorbike servicing has to be earlier than laundry, would have the same effect in determining the order of the student's activities?

   (A)   Laundry has to be one of the last three activities.
   (B)   Laundry has to be either immediately before or immediately after jogging.
   (C)   Jogging has to be earlier than laundry.
   (D)   Laundry has to be earlier than hedge trimming.
   (E)   Laundry has to be earlier than jogging.

GO ON TO THE NEXT PAGE.

Questions 6–11

Each of exactly three actors—Gombrich, Otto, and Raines—auditions for parts on exactly two of the following days of a particular week: Wednesday, Thursday, Friday, and Saturday. On each of these days at least one of the actors auditions for parts. The order of that week's auditions must meet the following conditions:

The first day on which Otto auditions is some day before the first day on which Raines auditions.

There is at least one day on which both Gombrich and Raines audition.

At least one of the actors auditions on both Thursday and Saturday.

6. Which one of the following could be an accurate matching of the actors to the days on which they audition?

- (A) Gombrich: Thursday, Friday
  Otto: Wednesday, Saturday
  Raines: Friday, Saturday
- (B) Gombrich: Thursday, Saturday
  Otto: Wednesday, Friday
  Raines: Friday, Saturday
- (C) Gombrich: Friday, Saturday
  Otto: Thursday, Saturday
  Raines: Wednesday, Friday
- (D) Gombrich: Wednesday, Thursday
  Otto: Wednesday, Saturday
  Raines: Thursday, Saturday
- (E) Gombrich: Wednesday, Friday
  Otto: Wednesday, Thursday
  Raines: Thursday, Saturday

7. If Otto auditions on both Thursday and Saturday, then Gombrich could audition on both

- (A) Wednesday and Thursday
- (B) Wednesday and Friday
- (C) Thursday and Friday
- (D) Thursday and Saturday
- (E) Friday and Saturday

8. Which one of the following CANNOT be true of the week's auditions?

- (A) Gombrich's last audition is on Thursday.
- (B) Gombrich's last audition is on Friday.
- (C) Otto's last audition is on Saturday.
- (D) Raines's last audition is on Friday.
- (E) Raines's last audition is on Thursday.

9. Which one of the following pairs of days CANNOT be the two days on which Otto auditions?

- (A) Wednesday and Thursday
- (B) Wednesday and Friday
- (C) Wednesday and Saturday
- (D) Thursday and Friday
- (E) Thursday and Saturday

10. Which one of the following could be true?

- (A) All three actors audition on Wednesday.
- (B) All three actors audition on Friday.
- (C) All three actors audition on Saturday.
- (D) Otto auditions on Friday and on Saturday.
- (E) Raines auditions on Wednesday and on Friday.

11. If Gombrich auditions on both Wednesday and Saturday, then which one of the following could be true?

- (A) Otto auditions on both Wednesday and Thursday.
- (B) Otto auditions on both Wednesday and Friday.
- (C) Otto auditions on both Wednesday and Saturday.
- (D) Raines auditions on both Wednesday and Saturday.
- (E) Raines auditions on both Thursday and Friday.

GO ON TO THE NEXT PAGE.

Questions 12–17

Each of seven toy dinosaurs—an iguanadon, a lambeosaur, a plateosaur, a stegosaur, a tyrannosaur, an ultrasaur, and a velociraptor—is completely colored either green, mauve, red, or yellow. A display is to consist entirely of exactly five of these toys. The display must meet the following specifications:

  Exactly two mauve toys are included.
  The stegosaur is red and is included.
  The iguanadon is included only if it is green.
  The plateosaur is included only if it is yellow.
  The velociraptor is included only if the ultrasaur is not.
  If both the lambeosaur and the ultrasaur are included, at least one of them is not mauve.

12. Which one of the following could be the toys included in the display?

   (A) the lambeosaur, the plateosaur, the stegosaur, the ultrasaur, the velociraptor
   (B) the lambeosaur, the plateosaur, the stegosaur, the tyrannosaur, the ultrasaur
   (C) the iguanadon, the lambeosaur, the plateosaur, the stegosaur, the ultrasaur
   (D) the iguanadon, the lambeosaur, the plateosaur, the tyrannosaur, the velociraptor
   (E) the iguanadon, the lambeosaur, the stegosaur, the ultrasaur, the velociraptor

13. If the tyrannosaur is not included in the display, then the display must contain each of the following EXCEPT:

   (A) a green iguanadon
   (B) a mauve velociraptor
   (C) a mauve lambeosaur
   (D) a mauve ultrasaur
   (E) a yellow plateosaur

14. Which one of the following is a pair of toys that could be included in the display together?

   (A) a green lambeosaur and a mauve velociraptor
   (B) a green lambeosaur and a yellow tyrannosaur
   (C) a green lambeosaur and a yellow ultrasaur
   (D) a yellow tyrannosaur and a green ultrasaur
   (E) a yellow tyrannosaur and a red velociraptor

15. If the display includes a yellow tyrannosaur, then which one of the following must be true?

   (A) The iguanadon is included in the display.
   (B) The plateosaur is not included in the display.
   (C) The display includes two yellow toy dinosaurs.
   (D) The display contains a green lambeosaur.
   (E) The display contains a mauve velociraptor.

16. If both the iguanadon and the ultrasaur are included in the display, then the display must contain which one of the following?

   (A) a mauve tyrannosaur
   (B) a mauve ultrasaur
   (C) a yellow lambeosaur
   (D) a yellow plateosaur
   (E) a yellow ultrasaur

17. If the display includes two green toys, then which one of the following could be true?

   (A) There is exactly one yellow toy included in the display.
   (B) The tyrannosaur is included in the display and it is green.
   (C) Neither the lambeosaur nor the velociraptor is included in the display.
   (D) Neither the tyrannosaur nor the velociraptor is included in the display.
   (E) Neither the ultrasaur nor the velociraptor is included in the display.

GO ON TO THE NEXT PAGE.

Questions 18–23

A charitable foundation awards grants in exactly four areas—medical services, theater arts, wildlife preservation, and youth services—each grant being in one of these areas. One or more grants are awarded in each of the four quarters of a calendar year. Additionally, over the course of a calendar year, the following must obtain:

Grants are awarded in all four areas.
No more than six grants are awarded.
No grants in the same area are awarded in the same quarter or in consecutive quarters.
Exactly two medical services grants are awarded.
A wildlife preservation grant is awarded in the second quarter.

18. Which one of the following is a possible allocation of grants in a particular calendar year?

(A) first quarter: theater arts
second quarter: wildlife preservation
third quarter: medical services, youth services
fourth quarter: theater arts
(B) first quarter: wildlife preservation
second quarter: medical services
third quarter: theater arts
fourth quarter: medical services, youth services
(C) first quarter: youth services
second quarter: wildlife preservation, medical services
third quarter: theater arts
fourth quarter: medical services, youth services
(D) first quarter: medical services, theater arts
second quarter: theater arts, wildlife preservation
third quarter: youth services
fourth quarter: medical services
(E) first quarter: medical services, theater arts
second quarter: wildlife preservation, youth services
third quarter: theater arts
fourth quarter: medical services, youth services

19. Which one of the following CANNOT be true in a particular calendar year?

(A) In each of the two quarters in which a medical services grant is awarded, no other grant is awarded.
(B) Exactly two theater arts grants are awarded, one in the second quarter and one in the fourth quarter.
(C) Exactly two youth services grants are awarded, one in the first quarter and one in the third quarter.
(D) Two wildlife preservation grants and two youth services grants are awarded.
(E) Three grants are awarded in the fourth quarter.

20. If a wildlife preservation grant and a youth services grant are awarded in the same quarter of a particular calendar year, then any of the following could be true that year EXCEPT:

(A) A medical services grant is awarded in the second quarter.
(B) A theater arts grant is awarded in the first quarter.
(C) A theater arts grant is awarded in the second quarter.
(D) A wildlife preservation grant is awarded in the fourth quarter.
(E) A youth services grant is awarded in the third quarter.

21. If exactly two grants are awarded in just one of the four quarters of a particular calendar year, then which one of the following could be true that year?

(A) Two youth services grants are awarded.
(B) Neither a medical services grant nor a youth services grant is awarded in the first quarter.
(C) A wildlife preservation grant is awarded in the fourth quarter.
(D) Both a youth services grant and a theater arts grant are awarded in the first quarter.
(E) A youth services grant is awarded in the first quarter and a theater arts grant is awarded in the second quarter.

22. Which one of the following CANNOT be true in a particular calendar year?

(A) Three grants are awarded in a quarter, none of which is a medical services grant.
(B) Exactly two grants are awarded in the first quarter and exactly two in the third quarter.
(C) Exactly two grants are awarded in the first quarter and exactly two in the fourth quarter.
(D) Theater arts grants are awarded in the first and fourth quarters, and no other grants are awarded in those two quarters.
(E) Wildlife preservation grants are awarded in the second and fourth quarters, and no other grants are awarded in those two quarters.

23. It is fully determined which grants are awarded for each quarter of a particular calendar year if which one of the following is true that year?

(A) Two theater arts grants are awarded.
(B) Two youth services grants are awarded.
(C) Three grants are awarded in the first quarter.
(D) Three grants are awarded in the second quarter.
(E) Three grants are awarded in the third quarter.

S T O P

IF YOU FINISH BEFORE TIME IS CALLED, YOU MAY CHECK YOUR WORK ON THIS SECTION ONLY.
DO NOT WORK ON ANY OTHER SECTION IN THE TEST.

SECTION II

Time—35 minutes

26 Questions

Directions: The questions in this section are based on the reasoning contained in brief statements or passages. For some questions, more than one of the choices could conceivably answer the question. However, you are to choose the best answer; that is, the response that most accurately and completely answers the question. You should not make assumptions that are by commonsense standards implausible, superfluous, or incompatible with the passage. After you have chosen the best answer, blacken the corresponding space on your answer sheet.

1. Many doctors cater to patients' demands that they be prescribed antibiotics for their colds. However, colds are caused by viruses, and antibiotics have no effect on viruses, and so antibiotics have no effect on colds. Such treatments are also problematic because antibiotics can have dangerous side effects. So doctors should never prescribe antibiotics to treat colds.

The reasoning above most closely conforms to which one of the following principles?

(A) A doctor should not prescribe a drug for a condition if it cannot improve that condition and if the drug potentially has adverse side effects.

(B) A doctor should not prescribe any drug that might have harmful effects on the patient even if the drug might have a positive effect on the patient.

(C) A doctor should attempt to prescribe every drug that is likely to affect the patient's health positively.

(D) A doctor should withhold treatment from a patient if the doctor is uncertain whether the treatment will benefit the patient.

(E) A doctor should never base the decision to prescribe a certain medication for a patient on the patient's claims about the effectiveness of that medication.

2. Long-distance runners use two different kinds of cognitive strategies: "associative" and "dissociative." Associative strategies involve attending closely to physical sensations, while dissociative strategies involve mostly ignoring physical sensations. Associative strategies, unlike dissociative ones, require so much concentration that they result in mental exhaustion lasting more than a day. Since it is important for long-distance runners to enter a race mentally refreshed, _____.

Which one of the following most logically completes the argument?

(A) long-distance runners should not rely heavily on associative strategies during training the day before they run in a race

(B) unless they regularly train using associative strategies, long-distance runners should use dissociative strategies during races

(C) maximizing the benefits of training for long-distance running involves frequently alternating associative and dissociative strategies

(D) long-distance runners are about evenly divided between those who use dissociative strategies during races and those who use associative strategies during races

(E) in long-distance running, dissociative strategies are generally more effective for a day's training run than are associative strategies

GO ON TO THE NEXT PAGE.

3. MetroBank made loans to ten small companies, in amounts ranging from $1,000 to $100,000. These ten loans all had graduated payment plans, i.e., the scheduled monthly loan payment increased slightly each month over the five-year term of the loan. Nonetheless, the average payment received by MetroBank for these ten loans had decreased by the end of the five-year term.

Which one of the following, if true, most helps to resolve the apparent discrepancy in the statements above?

(A) The number of small companies receiving new loans from MetroBank increased over the five-year term.

(B) Several of the ten small companies also borrowed money from other banks.

(C) Most banks offer a greater number of loans for under $100,000 than for over $100,000.

(D) Of the ten small companies, the three that had borrowed the largest amounts paid off their loans within three years.

(E) For some loans made by MetroBank, the monthly payment decreases slightly over the term of the loan.

4. Professor: A guest speaker recently delivered a talk entitled "The Functions of Democratic Governments" to a Political Ideologies class at this university. The talk was carefully researched and theoretical in nature. But two students who disagreed with the theory hurled vicious taunts at the speaker. Several others applauded their attempt to humiliate the speaker. This incident shows that universities these days do not foster fair-minded and tolerant intellectual debate.

The professor's reasoning is flawed in that it

(A) draws a conclusion based on the professor's own opinion rather than on that of the majority of the students present at the talk

(B) is inconsistent in advocating tolerance while showing intolerance of the dissenting students' views

(C) relies primarily on an emotional appeal

(D) draws a general conclusion based on too small a sample

(E) incorrectly focuses on the behavior of the dissenting students rather than relating the reasons for that behavior

5. Studies reveal that most people select the foods they eat primarily on the basis of flavor, and that nutrition is usually a secondary concern at best. This suggests that health experts would have more success in encouraging people to eat wholesome foods if they emphasized how flavorful those foods truly are rather than how nutritious they are.

Which one of the following, if true, most strengthens the argument above?

(A) Most people currently believe that wholesome foods are more flavorful, on average, than unwholesome foods are.

(B) Few people, when given a choice between foods that are flavorful but not nutritious and foods that are nutritious but not flavorful, will choose the foods that are nutritious but not flavorful.

(C) Health experts' attempts to encourage people to eat wholesome foods by emphasizing how nutritious those foods are have been moderately successful.

(D) The studies that revealed that people choose the foods they eat primarily on the basis of flavor also revealed that people rated as most flavorful those foods that were least nutritious.

(E) In a study, subjects who were told that a given food was very flavorful were more willing to try the food and more likely to enjoy it than were subjects who were told that the food was nutritious.

GO ON TO THE NEXT PAGE.

6. Studies show that individuals with a high propensity for taking risks tend to have fewer ethical principles to which they consciously adhere in their business interactions than do most people. On the other hand, individuals with a strong desire to be accepted socially tend to have more such principles than do most people. And, in general, the more ethical principles to which someone consciously adheres, the more ethical is that person's behavior. Therefore, business schools can promote more ethical behavior among future businesspeople by promoting among their students the desire to be accepted socially and discouraging the propensity for taking risks.

The reasoning in the argument is flawed because the argument

(A) infers from the fact that something is usually true that it is always true
(B) takes for granted that promoting ethical behavior is more important than any other goal
(C) concludes merely from the fact that two things are correlated that one causes the other
(D) takes for granted that certain actions are morally wrong simply because most people believe that they are morally wrong
(E) draws a conclusion that simply restates a claim presented in support of that conclusion

7. Essayist: Lessing contended that an art form's medium dictates the kind of representation the art form must employ in order to be legitimate; painting, for example, must represent simultaneous arrays of colored shapes, while literature, consisting of words read in succession, must represent events or actions occurring in sequence. The claim about literature must be rejected, however, if one regards as legitimate the imagists' poems, which consist solely of amalgams of disparate images.

Which one of the following, if assumed, enables the essayist's conclusion to be properly drawn?

(A) An amalgam of disparate images cannot represent a sequence of events or actions.
(B) Poems whose subject matter is not appropriate to their medium are illegitimate.
(C) Lessing was not aware that the imagists' poetry consists of an amalgam of disparate images.
(D) All art, even the imagists' poetry, depicts or represents some subject matter.
(E) All art represents something either as simultaneous or as successive.

8. A psychiatrist argued that there is no such thing as a multiple personality disorder on the grounds that in all her years of clinical practice, she had never encountered one case of this type.

Which one of the following most closely parallels the questionable reasoning cited above?

(A) Anton concluded that colds are seldom fatal on the grounds that in all his years of clinical practice, he never had a patient who died of a cold.
(B) Lyla said that no one in the area has seen a groundhog and so there are probably no groundhogs in the area.
(C) Sauda argued that because therapy rarely had an effect on her patient's type of disorder, therapy was not warranted.
(D) Thomas argued that because Natasha has driven her car to work every day since she bought it, she would probably continue to drive her car to work.
(E) Jerod had never spotted a deer in his area and concluded from this that there are no deer in the area.

9. Even if many more people in the world excluded meat from their diet, world hunger would not thereby be significantly reduced.

Which one of the following, if true, most calls into question the claim above?

(A) Hunger often results from natural disasters like typhoons or hurricanes, which sweep away everything in their path.
(B) Both herds and crops are susceptible to devastating viral and other diseases.
(C) The amount of land needed to produce enough meat to feed one person for a week can grow enough grain to feed more than ten people for a week.
(D) Often people go hungry because they live in remote barren areas where there is no efficient distribution for emergency food relief.
(E) Most historical cases of famine have been due to bad social and economic policies or catastrophes such as massive crop failure.

GO ON TO THE NEXT PAGE.

10. Dairy farmer: On our farm, we have great concern for our cows' environmental conditions. We have recently made improvements that increase their comfort, such as providing them with special sleeping mattresses. These changes are intended to increase blood flow to the udder. This increased blood flow would boost milk output and thus increase profits.

Of the following propositions, which one is best illustrated by the dairy farmer's statements?

(A) Dairy cows cannot have comfortable living conditions unless farmers have some knowledge about the physiology of milk production.
(B) Farming practices introduced for the sake of maximizing profits can improve the living conditions of farm animals.
(C) More than other farm animals, dairy cows respond favorably to improvements in their living environments.
(D) The productivity of dairy farms should be increased only if the quality of the product is not compromised.
(E) The key to maximizing profits on a dairy farm is having a concern for dairy cows' environment.

11. Pat: E-mail fosters anonymity, which removes barriers to self-revelation. This promotes a degree of intimacy with strangers that would otherwise take years of direct personal contact to attain.

Amar: Frankness is not intimacy. Intimacy requires a real social bond, and social bonds cannot be formed without direct personal contact.

The dialogue most strongly supports the claim that Pat and Amar disagree with each other about whether

(A) barriers to self-revelation hinder the initial growth of intimacy
(B) E-mail can increase intimacy between friends
(C) intimacy between those who communicate with each other solely by e-mail is possible
(D) real social bonds always lead to intimacy
(E) the use of e-mail removes barriers to self-revelation

12. Criminologist: The main purpose of most criminal organizations is to generate profits. The ongoing revolutions in biotechnology and information technology promise to generate enormous profits. Therefore, criminal organizations will undoubtedly try to become increasingly involved in these areas.

The conclusion of the criminologist's argument is properly inferred if which one of the following is assumed?

(A) If an organization tries to become increasingly involved in areas that promise to generate enormous profits, then the main purpose of that organization is to generate profits.
(B) At least some criminal organizations are or will at some point become aware that the ongoing revolutions in biotechnology and information technology promise to generate enormous profits.
(C) Criminal organizations are already heavily involved in every activity that promises to generate enormous profits.
(D) Any organization whose main purpose is to generate profits will try to become increasingly involved in any technological revolution that promises to generate enormous profits.
(E) Most criminal organizations are willing to become involved in legal activities if those activities are sufficiently profitable.

13. Administrators of educational institutions are enthusiastic about the educational use of computers because they believe that it will enable schools to teach far more courses with far fewer teachers than traditional methods allow. Many teachers fear computers for the same reason. But this reason is mistaken. Computerized instruction requires more, not less, time of instructors, which indicates that any reduction in the number of teachers would require an accompanying reduction in courses offered.

The statement that the educational use of computers enables schools to teach far more courses with far fewer teachers figures in the argument in which one of the following ways?

(A) It is presented as a possible explanation for an observation that follows it.
(B) It is a statement of the problem the argument sets out to solve.
(C) It is a statement that the argument is designed to refute.
(D) It is a statement offered in support of the argument's main conclusion.
(E) It is the argument's main conclusion.

GO ON TO THE NEXT PAGE.

14. Scientists have shown that older bees, which usually forage outside the hive for food, tend to have larger brains than do younger bees, which usually do not forage but instead remain in the hive to tend to newly hatched bees. Since foraging requires greater cognitive ability than does tending to newly hatched bees, it appears that foraging leads to the increased brain size of older bees.

Which one of the following, if true, most seriously weakens the argument above?

(A) Bees that have foraged for a long time do not have significantly larger brains than do bees that have foraged for a shorter time.

(B) The brains of older bees that stop foraging to take on other responsibilities do not become smaller after they stop foraging.

(C) Those bees that travel a long distance to find food do not have significantly larger brains than do bees that locate food nearer the hive.

(D) In some species of bees, the brains of older bees are only marginally larger than those of younger bees.

(E) The brains of older bees that never learn to forage are the same size as those of their foraging counterparts of the same age.

15. Carla: Professors at public universities should receive paid leaves of absence to allow them to engage in research. Research not only advances human knowledge, but also improves professors' teaching by keeping them abreast of the latest information in their fields.

David: But even if you are right about the beneficial effects of research, why should our limited resources be devoted to supporting professors taking time off from teaching?

David's response to Carla is most vulnerable to criticism on the grounds that it

(A) ignores the part of Carla's remarks that could provide an answer to David's question

(B) takes for granted that the only function of a university professor is teaching

(C) incorrectly takes Carla's remarks as claiming that all funding for professors comes from tax money

(D) takes for granted that providing the opportunity for research is the only function of paid leaves of absence

(E) presumes, without providing justification, that professors do not need vacations

16. Software reviewer: Dictation software allows a computer to produce a written version of sentences that are spoken to it. Although dictation software has been promoted as a labor-saving invention, it fails to live up to its billing. The laborious part of writing is in the thinking and the editing, not in the typing. And proofreading the software's error-filled output generally squanders any time saved in typing.

Which one of the following most accurately describes the role played in the software reviewer's argument by the claim that dictation software fails to live up to its billing?

(A) It is the argument's main conclusion but not its only conclusion.

(B) It is the argument's only conclusion.

(C) It is an intermediate conclusion that is offered as direct support for the argument's main conclusion.

(D) It is a premise offered in support of the argument's conclusion.

(E) It is a premise offered as direct support for an intermediate conclusion of the argument.

GO ON TO THE NEXT PAGE.

17. Poetry journal patron: Everybody who publishes in *The Brick Wall Review* has to agree in advance that if a poem is printed in one of its regular issues, the magazine also has the right to reprint it, without monetary compensation, in its annual anthology. *The Brick Wall Review* makes enough money from sales of its anthologies to cover most operating expenses. So, if your magazine also published an anthology of poems first printed in your magazine, you could depend less on donations. After all, most poems published in your magazine are very similar to those published in *The Brick Wall Review*.

Which one of the following, if true, most weakens the patron's argument?

(A)   Neither *The Brick Wall Review* nor the other magazine under discussion depends on donations to cover most operating expenses.

(B)   Many of the poets whose work appears in *The Brick Wall Review* have had several poems rejected for publication by the other magazine under discussion.

(C)   The only compensation poets receive for publishing in the regular issues of the magazines under discussion are free copies of the issues in which their poems appear.

(D)   *The Brick Wall Review* depends on donations to cover most operating expenses not covered by income from anthology sales.

(E)   *The Brick Wall Review*'s annual poetry anthology always contains a number of poems by famous poets not published in the regular issues of the magazine.

18. No one with a serious medical problem would rely on the average person to prescribe treatment. Similarly, since a good public servant has the interest of the public at heart, _____.

Which one of the following statements would most reasonably complete the argument?

(A)   public servants should not be concerned about the outcomes of public opinion surveys

(B)   the average public servant knows more about what is best for society than the average person does

(C)   public servants should be more knowledgeable about the public good than they are

(D)   public servants should base decisions on something other than the average person's recommendations

(E)   one is a good public servant if one is more knowledgeable about the public good than is the average person

19. Team captain: Winning requires the willingness to cooperate, which in turn requires motivation. So you will not win if you are not motivated.

The pattern of reasoning in which one of the following is most similar to that in the argument above?

(A)   Being healthy requires exercise. But exercising involves risk of injury. So, paradoxically, anyone who wants to be healthy will not exercise.

(B)   Learning requires making some mistakes. And you must learn if you are to improve. So you will not make mistakes without there being a noticeable improvement.

(C)   Our political party will retain its status only if it raises more money. But raising more money requires increased campaigning. So our party will not retain its status unless it increases its campaigning.

(D)   You can repair your own bicycle only if you are enthusiastic. And if you are enthusiastic, you will also have mechanical aptitude. So if you are not able to repair your own bicycle, you lack mechanical aptitude.

(E)   Getting a ticket requires waiting in line. Waiting in line requires patience. So if you do not wait in line, you lack patience.

20. In the past, when there was no highway speed limit, the highway accident rate increased yearly, peaking a decade ago. At that time, the speed limit on highways was set at 90 kilometers per hour (kph) (55 miles per hour). Every year since the introduction of the highway speed limit, the highway accident rate has been at least 15 percent lower than that of its peak rate. Thus, setting the highway speed limit at 90 kph (55 mph) has reduced the highway accident rate by at least 15 percent.

Which one of the following, if true, most seriously weakens the argument?

(A) In the years prior to the introduction of the highway speed limit, many cars could go faster than 90 kph (55 mph).

(B) Ten years ago, at least 95 percent of all automobile accidents in the area occurred on roads with a speed limit of under 80 kph (50 mph).

(C) Although the speed limit on many highways is officially set at 90 kph (55 mph), most people typically drive faster than the speed limit.

(D) Thanks to changes in automobile design in the past ten years, drivers are better able to maintain control of their cars in dangerous situations.

(E) It was not until shortly after the introduction of the highway speed limit that most cars were equipped with features such as seat belts and airbags designed to prevent harm to passengers.

21. Editorial: It is a travesty of justice, social critics say, that we can launch rockets into outer space but cannot solve social problems that have plagued humanity. The assumption underlying this assertion is that there are greater difficulties involved in a space launch than are involved in ending long-standing social problems, which in turn suggests that a government's failure to achieve the latter is simply a case of misplaced priorities. The criticism is misplaced, however, for rocket technology is much simpler than the human psyche, and until we adequately understand the human psyche we cannot solve the great social problems.

The statement that rocket technology is much simpler than the human psyche plays which one of the following roles in the editorial's argument?

(A) It is cited as a possible objection to the argument's conclusion.

(B) According to the argument, it is a fact that has misled some social critics.

(C) It is the argument's conclusion.

(D) It is claimed to be a false assumption on which the reasoning that the argument seeks to undermine rests.

(E) It is used by the argument to attempt to undermine the reasoning behind a viewpoint.

22. Archaeologist: After the last ice age, groups of paleohumans left Siberia and crossed the Bering land bridge, which no longer exists, into North America. Archaeologists have discovered in Siberia a cache of Clovis points—the distinctive stone spear points made by paleohumans. This shows that, contrary to previous belief, the Clovis point was not invented in North America.

Which one of the following, if true, would most strengthen the archaeologist's argument?

(A) The Clovis points found in Siberia are older than any of those that have been found in North America.

(B) The Bering land bridge disappeared before any of the Clovis points found to date were made.

(C) Clovis points were more effective hunting weapons than earlier spear points had been.

(D) Archaeologists have discovered in Siberia artifacts that date from after the time paleohumans left Siberia.

(E) Some paleohuman groups that migrated from Siberia to North America via the Bering land bridge eventually returned to Siberia.

GO ON TO THE NEXT PAGE.

23. Taxi drivers, whose income is based on the fares they receive, usually decide when to finish work each day by setting a daily income target; they stop when they reach that target. This means that they typically work fewer hours on a busy day than on a slow day.

The facts described above provide the strongest evidence against which one of the following?

(A) The number of hours per day that a person is willing to work depends on that person's financial needs.

(B) People work longer when their effective hourly wage is high than when it is low.

(C) Workers will accept a lower hourly wage in exchange for the freedom to set their own schedules.

(D) People are willing to work many hours a day in order to avoid a reduction in their standard of living.

(E) People who are paid based on their production work more efficiently than those who are paid a fixed hourly wage.

24. Sometimes one reads a poem and believes that the poem expresses contradictory ideas, even if it is a great poem. So it is wrong to think that the meaning of a poem is whatever the author intends to communicate to the reader by means of the poem. No one who is writing a great poem intends it to communicate contradictory ideas.

Which one of the following is an assumption on which the argument depends?

(A) Different readers will usually disagree about what the author of a particular poem intends to communicate by means of that poem.

(B) If someone writes a great poem, he or she intends the poem to express one primary idea.

(C) Readers will not agree about the meaning of a poem if they do not agree about what the author of the poem intended the poem to mean.

(D) Anyone reading a great poem can discern every idea that the author intended to express in the poem.

(E) If a reader believes that a poem expresses a particular idea, then that idea is part of the meaning of the poem.

25. The law of the city of Weston regarding contributions to mayoral campaigns is as follows: all contributions to these campaigns in excess of $100 made by nonresidents of Weston who are not former residents of Weston must be registered with the city council. Brimley's mayoral campaign clearly complied with this law since it accepted contributions only from residents and former residents of Weston.

If all the statements above are true, which one of the following statements must be true?

(A) No nonresident of Weston contributed in excess of $100 to Brimley's campaign.

(B) Some contributions to Brimley's campaign in excess of $100 were registered with the city council.

(C) No contributions to Brimley's campaign needed to be registered with the city council.

(D) All contributions to Brimley's campaign that were registered with the city council were in excess of $100.

(E) Brimley's campaign did not register any contributions with the city council.

26. Historian: Flavius, an ancient Roman governor who believed deeply in the virtues of manual labor and moral temperance, actively sought to discourage the arts by removing state financial support for them. Also, Flavius was widely unpopular among his subjects, as we can conclude from the large number of satirical plays that were written about him during his administration.

The historian's argumentation is most vulnerable to criticism on the grounds that it

(A) fails to consider the percentage of plays written during Flavius's administration that were not explicitly about Flavius

(B) treats the satirical plays as a reliable indicator of Flavius's popularity despite potential bias on the part of the playwrights

(C) presumes, without providing evidence, that Flavius was unfavorably disposed toward the arts

(D) takes for granted that Flavius's attempt to discourage the arts was successful

(E) fails to consider whether manual labor and moral temperance were widely regarded as virtues in ancient Rome

S T O P

IF YOU FINISH BEFORE TIME IS CALLED, YOU MAY CHECK YOUR WORK ON THIS SECTION ONLY.
DO NOT WORK ON ANY OTHER SECTION IN THE TEST.

SECTION III
Time—35 minutes
25 Questions

Directions: The questions in this section are based on the reasoning contained in brief statements or passages. For some questions, more than one of the choices could conceivably answer the question. However, you are to choose the best answer; that is, the response that most accurately and completely answers the question. You should not make assumptions that are by commonsense standards implausible, superfluous, or incompatible with the passage. After you have chosen the best answer, blacken the corresponding space on your answer sheet.

1. Educators studied the performance of 200 students in a university's history classes. They found that those students who performed the best had either part-time jobs or full-time jobs, had their history classes early in the morning, and had a very limited social life, whereas those students who performed the worst had no jobs, had their history classes early in the morning, and had a very active social life.

   Which one of the following, if true, most helps to explain the educators' findings?

   (A) The students compensated for any study time lost due to their jobs but they did not compensate for any study time lost due to their social lives.
   (B) The students who had full-time jobs typically worked late-night hours at those jobs.
   (C) Better students tend to choose classes that are scheduled to meet early in the morning.
   (D) A larger percentage of those students interested in majoring in history had part-time jobs than had full-time jobs.
   (E) Although having a job tends to provide a release from stress, thus increasing academic performance, having a full-time job, like having an active social life, can distract a student from studying.

2. Politician: Most of those at the meeting were not persuaded by Kuyler's argument, nor should they have been, for Kuyler's argument implied that it would be improper to enter into a contract with the government; and yet—as many people know—Kuyler's company has had numerous lucrative contracts with the government.

   Which one of the following describes a flaw in the politician's argument?

   (A) It concludes that an argument is defective merely on the grounds that the argument has failed to persuade anyone of the truth of its conclusion.
   (B) It relies on testimony that is likely to be biased.
   (C) It rejects an argument merely on the grounds that the arguer has not behaved in a way that is consistent with the argument.
   (D) It rejects a position merely on the grounds that an inadequate argument has been given for it.
   (E) It rejects an argument on the basis of an appeal to popular opinion.

3. Although free international trade allows countries to specialize, which in turn increases productivity, such specialization carries risks. After all, small countries often rely on one or two products for the bulk of their exports. If those products are raw materials, the supply is finite and can be used up. If they are foodstuffs, a natural disaster can wipe out a season's production overnight.

   Which one of the following most accurately expresses the conclusion of the argument as a whole?

   (A) Specialization within international trade comes with risks.
   (B) A natural disaster can destroy a whole season's production overnight, devastating a small country's economy.
   (C) A small country's supply of raw materials can be used up in a short period.
   (D) Some countries rely on a small number of products for the export-based sectors of their economies.
   (E) When international trade is free, countries can specialize in what they export.

GO ON TO THE NEXT PAGE.

4. Two randomly selected groups of 30 adults each were asked to write short stories on a particular topic. One group was told that the best stories would be awarded cash prizes, while the other group was not told of any prizes. Each story was evaluated by a team of judges who were given no indication of the group from which the story came. The stories submitted by those who thought they were competing for prizes were ranked on average significantly lower than the stories from the other group.

Which one of the following, if true, most helps to explain the difference in average ranking between the two groups' stories?

(A) The cash prizes were too small to motivate an average adult to make a significant effort to produce stories of high quality.

(B) People writing to win prizes show a greater than usual tendency to produce stereotypical stories that show little creativity.

(C) Most adults show little originality in writing stories on a topic suggested by someone else.

(D) The team of judges was biased in favor of stories that they judged to be more realistic.

(E) No one explained clearly to either group what standards would be used in judging their stories.

5. Hernandez: I recommend that staff cars be replaced every four years instead of every three years. Three-year-old cars are still in good condition and this would result in big savings.

Green: I disagree. Some of our salespeople with big territories wear out their cars in three years.

Hernandez: I meant three-year-old cars subjected to normal use.

In the conversation, Hernandez responds to Green's objection in which one of the following ways?

(A) by explicitly qualifying a premise used earlier

(B) by criticizing salespeople who wear out their cars in three years

(C) by disputing the accuracy of Green's evidence

(D) by changing the subject to the size of sales territories

(E) by indicating that Green used a phrase ambiguously

6. Economist: As should be obvious, raising the minimum wage significantly would make it more expensive for businesses to pay workers for minimum-wage jobs. Therefore, businesses could not afford to continue to employ as many workers for such jobs. So raising the minimum wage significantly will cause an increase in unemployment.

Which one of the following, if true, most weakens the economist's argument?

(A) Businesses typically pass the cost of increased wages on to consumers without adversely affecting profits.

(B) When the difference between minimum wage and a skilled worker's wage is small, a greater percentage of a business's employees will be skilled workers.

(C) A modest increase in unemployment is acceptable because the current minimum wage is not a livable wage.

(D) Most workers are earning more than the current minimum wage.

(E) The unemployment rate has been declining steadily in recent years.

7. Scientists removed all viruses from a seawater sample and then measured the growth rate of the plankton population in the water. They expected the rate to increase dramatically, but the population actually got smaller.

Which one of the following, if true, most helps to explain the unexpected result described above?

(A) Viruses in seawater help to keep the plankton population below the maximum level that the resources in the water will support.

(B) Plankton and viruses in seawater compete for some of the same nutrients.

(C) Plankton utilize the nutrients released by the death of organisms killed by viruses.

(D) The absence of viruses can facilitate the flourishing of bacteria that sometimes damage other organisms.

(E) At any given time, a considerable portion of the plankton in seawater are already infected by viruses.

GO ON TO THE NEXT PAGE.

8. City council member: The Senior Guild has asked for a temporary exception to the ordinance prohibiting automobiles in municipal parks. Their case does appear to deserve the exception. However, if we grant this exception, we will find ourselves granting many other exceptions to this ordinance, some of which will be undeserved. Before long, we will be granting exceptions to all manner of other city ordinances. If we are to prevent anarchy in our city, we must deny the Senior Guild's request.

The city council member's argument is most vulnerable to criticism on the grounds that it

(A) distorts an argument and then attacks this distorted argument
(B) dismisses a claim because of its source rather than because of its content
(C) presumes, without sufficient warrant, that one event will lead to a particular causal sequence of events
(D) contains premises that contradict one another
(E) fails to make a needed distinction between deserved exceptions and undeserved ones

9. Physician: In comparing our country with two other countries of roughly the same population size, I found that even though we face the same dietary, bacterial, and stress-related causes of ulcers as they do, prescriptions for ulcer medicines in all socioeconomic strata are much rarer here than in those two countries. It's clear that we suffer significantly fewer ulcers, per capita, than they do.

Which one of the following, if true, most strengthens the physician's argument?

(A) The two countries that were compared with the physician's country had approximately the same ulcer rates as each other.
(B) The people of the physician's country have a cultural tradition of stoicism that encourages them to ignore physical ailments rather than to seek remedies for them.
(C) Several other countries not covered in the physician's comparisons have more prescriptions for ulcer medication than does the physician's country.
(D) A person in the physician's country who is suffering from ulcers is just as likely to obtain a prescription for the ailment as is a person suffering from ulcers in one of the other two countries.
(E) The physician's country has a much better system for reporting the number of prescriptions of a given type that are obtained each year than is present in either of the other two countries.

10. Columnist: The failure of bicyclists to obey traffic regulations is a causal factor in more than one quarter of the traffic accidents involving bicycles. Since inadequate bicycle safety equipment is also a factor in more than a quarter of such accidents, bicyclists are at least partially responsible for more than half of the traffic accidents involving bicycles.

The columnist's reasoning is flawed in that it

(A) presumes, without providing justification, that motorists are a factor in less than half of the traffic accidents involving bicycles
(B) improperly infers the presence of a causal connection on the basis of a correlation
(C) fails to consider the possibility that more than one factor may contribute to a given accident
(D) fails to provide the source of the figures it cites
(E) fails to consider that the severity of injuries to bicyclists from traffic accidents can vary widely

11. Many vaccines create immunity to viral diseases by introducing a certain portion of the disease-causing virus's outer coating into the body. Exposure to that part of a virus is as effective as exposure to the whole virus in stimulating production of antibodies that will subsequently recognize and kill the whole virus. To create a successful vaccine of this type, doctors must first isolate in the disease-causing virus a portion that stimulates antibody production. Now that a suitable portion of the virus that causes hepatitis E has been isolated, doctors claim they can produce a vaccine that will produce permanent immunity to that disease.

Which one of the following, if true, most strongly counters the doctors' claim?

(A) Most of the people who contract hepatitis E are young adults who were probably exposed to the virus in childhood also.
(B) Some laboratory animals exposed to one strain of the hepatitis virus developed immunity to all strains of the virus.
(C) Researchers developed a successful vaccine for another strain of hepatitis, hepatitis B, after first isolating the virus that causes it.
(D) The virus that causes hepatitis E is very common in some areas, so the number of people exposed to that virus is likely to be quite high in those areas.
(E) Many children who are exposed to viruses that cause childhood diseases such as chicken pox never develop those diseases.

GO ON TO THE NEXT PAGE.

12. Editorial: To qualify as an effective law, as opposed to merely an impressive declaration, a command must be backed up by an effective enforcement mechanism. That is why societies have police. The power of the police to enforce a society's laws makes those laws effective. But there is currently no international police force. Hence, what is called "international law" is not effective law.

Which one of the following is an assumption required by the editorial's argument?

(A) No one obeys a command unless mechanisms exist to compel obedience.

(B) If an international police force were established, then so-called international law would become effective law.

(C) The only difference between international law and the law of an individual society is the former's lack of an effective enforcement mechanism.

(D) The primary purpose of a police force is to enforce the laws of the society.

(E) Only an international police force could effectively enforce international law.

13. Art historian: More than any other genre of representational painting, still-life painting lends itself naturally to art whose goal is the artist's self-expression, rather than merely the reflection of a preexisting external reality. This is because in still-life painting, the artist invariably chooses, modifies, and arranges the objects to be painted. Thus, the artist has considerably more control over the composition and subject of a still-life painting than over those of a landscape painting or portrait, for example.

Which one of the following is most strongly supported by the art historian's statements?

(A) Landscape painting and portraiture are the artistic genres that lend themselves most naturally to the mere reflection of a preexisting external reality.

(B) The only way in which artists control the composition and subject of a painting is by choosing, modifying, and arranging the objects to be represented in that painting.

(C) Nonrepresentational painting does not lend itself as naturally as still-life painting does to the goal of the artist's self-expression.

(D) In genres of representational painting other than still-life painting, the artist does not always choose, modify, and arrange the objects to be painted.

(E) When painting a portrait, artists rarely attempt to express themselves through the choice, modification, or arrangement of the background elements against which the subject of the portrait is painted.

14. Food labeling regulation: Food of a type that does not ordinarily contain fat cannot be labeled "nonfat" unless most people mistakenly believe the food ordinarily contains fat. If most people mistakenly believe that a food ordinarily contains fat, the food may be labeled "nonfat" if the label also states that the food ordinarily contains no fat.

Which one of the following situations violates the food labeling regulation?

(A) Although most people know that bran flakes do not normally contain fat, Lester's Bran Flakes are not labeled "nonfat."

(B) Although most people are aware that lasagna ordinarily contains fat, Lester's Lasagna, which contains no fat, is not labeled "nonfat."

(C) Although most garlic baguettes contain fat, Lester's Garlic Baguettes are labeled "nonfat."

(D) Although most people are aware that applesauce does not ordinarily contain fat, Lester's Applesauce is labeled "nonfat."

(E) Although most people mistakenly believe that salsa ordinarily contains fat, the label on Lester's Zesty Salsa says "This product, like all salsas, is nonfat."

GO ON TO THE NEXT PAGE.

15. Medical ethicist: Assuming there is a reasonable chance for a cure, it is acceptable to offer experimental treatments for a disease to patients who suffer from extreme symptoms of that disease. Such patients are best able to weigh a treatment's risks against the benefits of a cure. Therefore, it is never acceptable to offer experimental treatments to patients who experience no extreme symptoms of the relevant disease.

The flawed reasoning in which one of the following is most similar to the flawed reasoning in the medical ethicist's argument?

(A) Even a geological engineer with a background in economics can lose money investing in mineral extraction. So, those who are less knowledgeable about geology or economics should not expect to make money in every investment in mineral extraction.

(B) One is always in a better position to judge whether an automobile would be worth its cost if one has test-driven that automobile. Therefore, if an automobile proves to be not worth its cost, it is likely that it was not test-driven.

(C) Someone born and raised in a country, who has lived abroad and then returned, is exceptionally qualified to judge the merits of living in that country. That is why someone who has not lived in that country should not form judgments about the merits of living there.

(D) One can never eliminate all of the risks of daily life, and even trying to avoid every risk in life is costly. Therefore, anyone who is reasonable will accept some of the risks of daily life.

(E) Almost any industrial development will have unwelcome environmental side effects. Therefore, it is not worthwhile to weigh the costs of potential environmental side effects since such side effects are unavoidable.

16. Critic: As modern methods of communication and transportation have continued to improve, the pace of life today has become faster than ever before. This speed has created feelings of impermanence and instability, making us feel as if we never have enough time to achieve what we want—or at least what we think we want.

The critic's statements most closely conform to which one of the following assessments?

(A) The fast pace of modern life has made it difficult for people to achieve their goals.

(B) The disadvantages of technological progress often outweigh the advantages.

(C) Changes in people's feelings about life can result from technological changes.

(D) The perception of impermanence in contemporary life makes it more difficult for people to know what they want.

(E) Changes in people's feelings fuel the need for technological advancement.

17. Consumer: If you buy a watch at a department store and use it only in the way it was intended to be used, but the watch stops working the next day, then the department store will refund your money. So by this very reasonable standard, Bingham's Jewelry Store should give me a refund even though they themselves are not a department store, since the watch I bought from them stopped working the very next day.

The consumer's argument relies on the assumption that

(A) one should not sell something unless one expects that it will function in the way it was originally designed to function

(B) a watch bought at a department store and a watch bought at Bingham's Jewelry Store can both be expected to keep working for about the same length of time if each is used only as it was intended to be used

(C) a seller should refund the money that was paid for a product if the product does not perform as the purchaser expected it to perform

(D) the consumer did not use the watch in a way contrary to the way it was intended to be used

(E) the watch that was purchased from Bingham's Jewelry Store was not a new watch

GO ON TO THE NEXT PAGE.

18. A study found that patients referred by their doctors to psychotherapists practicing a new experimental form of therapy made more progress with respect to their problems than those referred to psychotherapists practicing traditional forms of therapy. Therapists practicing the new form of therapy, therefore, are more effective than therapists practicing traditional forms.

Which one of the following most accurately describes a flaw in the argument?

(A) It ignores the possibility that therapists trained in traditional forms of therapy use the same techniques in treating their patients as therapists trained in the new form of therapy do.

(B) It ignores the possibility that the patients referred to therapists practicing the new form of therapy had problems more amenable to treatment than did those referred to therapists practicing traditional forms.

(C) It presumes, without providing justification, that any psychotherapist trained in traditional forms of therapy is untrained in the new form of therapy.

(D) It ignores the possibility that therapists practicing the new form of therapy systematically differ from therapists practicing traditional forms of therapy with regard to some personality attribute relevant to effective treatment.

(E) It presumes, without providing justification, that the personal rapport between therapist and patient has no influence on the effectiveness of the treatment the patient receives.

19. Essayist: One of the drawbacks of extreme personal and political freedom is that free choices are often made for the worst. To expect people to thrive when they are given the freedom to make unwise decisions is frequently unrealistic. Once people see the destructive consequences of extreme freedom, they may prefer to establish totalitarian political regimes that allow virtually no freedom. Thus, one should not support political systems that allow extreme freedom.

Which one of the following principles, if valid, most helps to justify the essayist's reasoning?

(A) One should not support any political system that will inevitably lead to the establishment of a totalitarian political regime.

(B) One should not expect everyone to thrive even in a political system that maximizes people's freedom in the long run.

(C) One should support only those political systems that give people the freedom to make wise choices.

(D) One should not support any political system whose destructive consequences could lead people to prefer totalitarian political regimes.

(E) One should not support any political system that is based on unrealistic expectations about people's behavior under that system.

GO ON TO THE NEXT PAGE.

20. Ethicist: Every moral action is the keeping of an agreement, and keeping an agreement is nothing more than an act of securing mutual benefit. Clearly, however, not all instances of agreement-keeping are moral actions. Therefore, some acts of securing mutual benefit are not moral actions.

The pattern of reasoning in which one of the following arguments is most similar to that in the ethicist's argument?

(A) All calculators are kinds of computers, and all computers are devices for automated reasoning. However, not all devices for automated reasoning are calculators. Therefore, some devices for automated reasoning are not computers.

(B) All exercise is beneficial, and all things that are beneficial promote health. However, not all things that are beneficial are forms of exercise. Therefore, some exercise does not promote health.

(C) All metaphors are comparisons, and not all comparisons are surprising. However, all metaphors are surprising. Therefore, some comparisons are not metaphors.

(D) All architecture is design and all design is art. However, not all design is architecture. Therefore, some art is not design.

(E) All books are texts, and all texts are documents. However, not all texts are books. Therefore, some documents are not books.

21. Sociologist: The more technologically advanced a society is, the more marked its members' resistance to technological innovations. This is not surprising, because the more technologically advanced a society is, the more aware its members are of technology's drawbacks. Specifically, people realize that sophisticated technologies deeply affect the quality of human relations.

The claim that the more technologically advanced a society is, the more aware its members are of technology's drawbacks plays which one of the following roles in the sociologist's argument?

(A) It is a conclusion supported by the claim that people realize that sophisticated technologies deeply affect the quality of human relations.

(B) It is offered as an explanation of why people's resistance to technological innovations is more marked the more technologically advanced the society in which they live is.

(C) It is a premise in support of the claim that the quality of human relations in technologically advanced societies is extremely poor.

(D) It is a generalization based on the claim that the more people resist technological innovations, the more difficult it is for them to adjust to those innovations.

(E) It is an example presented to illustrate the claim that resistance to technological innovations deeply affects the quality of human relations.

GO ON TO THE NEXT PAGE.

22. To win democratic elections that are not fully subsidized by the government, nonwealthy candidates must be supported by wealthy patrons. This makes plausible the belief that these candidates will compromise their views to win that support. But since the wealthy are dispersed among the various political parties in roughly equal proportion to their percentage in the overall population, this belief is false.

The argument is vulnerable to criticism on the grounds that it fails to consider that

(A)   the primary function of political parties in democracies whose governments do not subsidize elections might not be to provide a means of negating the influence of wealth on elections

(B)   in democracies in which elections are not fully subsidized by the government, positions endorsed by political parties might be much less varied than the positions taken by candidates

(C)   in democracies, government-subsidized elections ensure that the views expressed by the people who run for office might not be overly influenced by the opinions of the wealthiest people in those countries

(D)   in democracies in which elections are not fully subsidized by the government, it might be no easier for a wealthy person to win an election than it is for a nonwealthy person to win an election

(E)   a democracy in which candidates do not compromise their views in order to be elected to office might have other flaws

23. In modern "brushless" car washes, cloth strips called mitters have replaced brushes. Mitters are easier on most cars' finishes than brushes are. This is especially important with the new clear-coat finishes found on many cars today, which are more easily scratched than older finishes are.

Which one of the following is most strongly supported by the statements above, if those statements are true?

(A)   When car washes all used brushes rather than mitters, there were more cars on the road with scratched finishes than there are today.

(B)   Modern "brushless" car washes were introduced as a direct response to the use of clear-coat finishes on cars.

(C)   Modern "brushless" car washes usually do not produce visible scratches on cars with older finishes.

(D)   Brushes are more effective than mitters and are preferred for cleaning cars with older finishes.

(E)   More cars in use today have clear-coat finishes rather than older finishes.

24. It is widely believed that lancelets—small, primitive sea animals—do not have hearts. Each lancelet has a contracting vessel, but this vessel is considered an artery rather than a heart. However, this vessel is indeed a heart. After all, it strongly resembles the structure of the heart of certain other sea animals. Moreover, the muscular contractions in the lancelet's vessel closely resemble the muscular contractions of other animals' hearts.

The argument's conclusion follows logically if which one of the following is assumed?

(A)   Only animals that have contracting vessels have hearts.

(B)   Some primitive animals other than lancelets have what is widely held to be a heart.

(C)   A vessel whose structure and actions closely resemble those of other animal hearts is a heart.

(D)   For a vessel in an animal to be properly considered a heart, that vessel must undergo muscular contractions.

(E)   No animal that has a heart lacks an artery.

25. Manager: I recommend that our company reconsider the decision to completely abandon our allegedly difficult-to-use computer software and replace it companywide with a new software package advertised as more flexible and easier to use. Several other companies in our region officially replaced the software we currently use with the new package, and while their employees can all use the new software, unofficially many continue to use their former software as much as possible.

Which one of the following is most strongly supported by the manager's statements?

(A)   The current company software is as flexible as the proposed new software package.

(B)   The familiarity that employees have with a computer software package is a more important consideration in selecting software than flexibility or initial ease of use.

(C)   The employees of the manager's company would find that the new software package lacks some of the capabilities of the present software.

(D)   Adopting the new software package would create two classes of employees, those who can use it and those who cannot.

(E)   Many of the employees in the manager's company would not prefer the new software package to the software currently in use.

S T O P

SECTION IV

Time—35 minutes

27 Questions

Directions: Each set of questions in this section is based on a single passage or a pair of passages. The questions are to be answered on the basis of what is <u>stated</u> or <u>implied</u> in the passage or pair of passages. For some of the questions, more than one of the choices could conceivably answer the question. However, you are to choose the <u>best</u> answer; that is, the response that most accurately and completely answers the question, and blacken the corresponding space on your answer sheet.

The United States government agency responsible for overseeing television and radio broadcasting, the Federal Communications Commission (FCC), had an early history of addressing only the concerns of parties
(5)   with an economic interest in broadcasting—chiefly broadcasting companies. The rights of viewers and listeners were not recognized by the FCC, which regarded them merely as members of the public. Unless citizens' groups were applying for broadcasting
(10) licenses, citizens did not have the standing necessary to voice their views at an FCC hearing. Consequently, the FCC appeared to be exclusively at the service of the broadcasting industry.

A landmark case changed the course of that
(15) history. In 1964, a local television station in Jackson, Mississippi was applying for a renewal of its broadcasting license. The United Church of Christ, representing Jackson's African American population, petitioned the FCC for a hearing about the broadcasting
(20) policies of that station. The church charged that the station advocated racial segregation to the point of excluding news and programs supporting integration. Arguing that the church lacked the level of economic interest required for a hearing, the FCC rejected the
(25) petition, though it attempted to mollify the church by granting only a short-term, probationary renewal to the station. Further, the FCC claimed that since it accepted the church's contentions with regard to misconduct on the part of the broadcasters, no hearing was necessary.
(30) However, that decision raised a question: If the contentions concerning the station were accepted, why was its license renewed at all? The real reason for denying the church a hearing was more likely the prospect that citizens' groups representing community
(35) preferences would begin to enter the closed worlds of government and industry.

The church appealed the FCC's decision in court, and in 1967 was granted the right to a public hearing on the station's request for a long-term license. The
(40) hearing was to little avail: the FCC dismissed much of the public input and granted a full renewal to the station. The church appealed again, and this time the judge took the unprecedented step of revoking the station's license without remand to the FCC, ruling that the
(45) church members were performing a public service in voicing the legitimate concerns of the community and, as such, should be accorded the right to challenge the renewal of the station's broadcasting license.

The case established a formidable precedent for
(50) opening up to the public the world of broadcasting.

Subsequent rulings have supported the right of the public to question the performance of radio and television licensees before the FCC at renewal time every three years. Along with racial issues, a range of
(55) other matters—from the quality of children's programming and the portrayal of violence to equal time for opposing political viewpoints—are now discussed at licensing proceedings because of the church's intervention.

1. Which one of the following most accurately expresses the main point of the passage?

(A) Because of the efforts of a church group in challenging an FCC decision, public input is now considered in broadcast licensing proceedings.

(B) Court rulings have forced the FCC to abandon policies that appeared to encourage biased coverage of public issues.

(C) The history of the FCC is important because it explains why government agencies are now forced to respond to public input.

(D) Because it has begun to serve the interests of the public, the FCC is less responsive to the broadcasting industry.

(E) In response to pressure from citizens' groups, the FCC has decided to open its license renewal hearings to the public.

GO ON TO THE NEXT PAGE.

2. The author mentions some additional topics now discussed at FCC hearings (lines 54–59) primarily in order to

(A)   support the author's claim that the case helped to open up to the public the world of broadcasting

(B)   suggest the level of vigilance that citizens' groups must maintain with regard to broadcasters

(C)   provide an explanation of why the public is allowed to question the performance of broadcasters on such a frequent basis

(D)   illustrate other areas of misconduct with which the station discussed in the passage was charged

(E)   demonstrate that the station discussed in the passage was not the only one to fall short of its obligation to the public

3. Which one of the following statements is affirmed by the passage?

(A)   The broadcasting industry's economic goals can be met most easily by minimizing the attention given to the interests of viewers and listeners.

(B)   The FCC was advised by broadcasters to bar groups with no economic interest in broadcasting from hearings concerning the broadcasting industry.

(C)   The court ruled in the case brought by the United Church of Christ that the FCC had the ultimate authority to decide whether to renew a broadcaster's license.

(D)   Before the United Church of Christ won its case, the FCC would not allow citizens' groups to speak as members of the public at FCC hearings.

(E)   The case brought by the United Church of Christ represents the first time a citizens' group was successful in getting its concerns about government agencies addressed to its satisfaction.

4. Based on information presented in the passage, with which one of the following statements would the author be most likely to agree?

(A)   If the United Church of Christ had not pursued its case, the FCC would not have been aware of the television station's broadcasting policies.

(B)   By their very nature, industrial and business interests are opposed to public interests.

(C)   The recourse of a citizens' group to the courts represents an effective means of protecting public interests.

(D)   Governmental regulation cannot safeguard against individual businesses acting contrary to public interests.

(E)   The government cannot be trusted to favor the rights of the public over broadcasters' economic interests.

5. The passage suggests that which one of the following has been established by the case discussed in the third paragraph?

(A)   Broadcasters are legally obligated to hold regular meetings at which the public can voice its concerns about broadcasting policies.

(B)   Broadcasters are now required by the FCC to consult citizens' groups when making programming decisions.

(C)   Except in cases involving clear misconduct by a broadcaster, the FCC need not seek public input in licensing hearings.

(D)   When evaluating the performance of a broadcaster applying for a license renewal, the FCC must obtain information about the preferences of the public.

(E)   In FCC licensing proceedings, parties representing community preferences should be granted standing along with those with an economic interest in broadcasting.

GO ON TO THE NEXT PAGE.

An effort should be made to dispel the misunderstandings that still prevent the much-needed synthesis and mutual supplementation of science and the humanities. This reconciliation should not be too
(5) difficult once it is recognized that the separation is primarily the result of a basic misunderstanding of the philosophical foundations of both science and the humanities.

Some humanists still identify science with an
(10) absurd mechanistic reductionism. There are many who feel that the scientist is interested in nothing more than "bodies in motion," in the strictly mathematical, physical, and chemical laws that govern the material world. This is the caricature of science drawn by
(15) representatives of the humanities who are ignorant of the nature of modern science and also of the scientific outlook in philosophy. For example, it is claimed that science either ignores or explains away the most essential human values. Those who believe this also
(20) assert that there are aspects of the human mind, manifest especially in the domains of morality, religion, and the arts, that contain an irreducible spiritual element and for that reason can never be adequately explained by science.
(25) Some scientists, on the other hand, claim that the humanist is interested in nothing more than emotion and sentiment, exhibiting the vagrant fancies of an undisciplined mind. To such men and women the humanities are useless because they serve no immediate
(30) and technological function for the practical survival of human society in the material world. Such pragmatists believe that the areas of morality, religion, and the arts should have only a secondary importance in people's lives.
(35) Thus there are misconceptions among humanists and scientists alike that are in need of correction. This correction leads to a much more acceptable position that could be called "scientific humanism," attempting as it does to combine the common elements of both
(40) disciplines. Both science and the humanities attempt to describe and explain. It is true that they begin their descriptions and explanations at widely separated points, but the objectives remain the same: a clearer understanding of people and their world. In achieving
(45) this understanding, science in fact does not depend exclusively on measurable data, and the humanities in fact profit from attempts at controlled evaluation. Scientific humanism can combine the scientific attitude with an active interest in the whole scale of
(50) human values. If uninformed persons insist on viewing science as only materialistic and the humanities as only idealistic, a fruitful collaboration of both fields is unlikely. The combination of science and the humanities is, however, possible, even probable, if we
(55) begin by noting their common objectives, rather than seeing only their different means.

6. Which one of the following best describes the main idea of the passage?

(A) Scientists' failure to understand humanists hinders collaborations between the two groups.
(B) The materialism of science and the idealism of the humanities have both been beneficial to modern society.
(C) Technological development will cease if science and the humanities remain at odds with each other.
(D) The current relationship between science and the humanities is less cooperative than their relationship once was.
(E) A synthesis of science and the humanities is possible and much-needed.

7. Which one of the following would the author be most likely to characterize as an example of a misunderstanding of science by a humanist?

(A) Science encourages the view that emotions are inexplicable.
(B) Science arises out of practical needs but serves other needs as well.
(C) Science depends exclusively on measurable data to support its claims.
(D) Science recognizes an irreducible spiritual element that makes the arts inexplicable.
(E) Science encourages the use of description in the study of human values.

8. It can be inferred from the passage that the author would be most likely to agree with which one of the following statements?

(A) Scientific humanism is characterized by the extension of description and explanation from science to the humanities.
(B) A clearer understanding of people is an objective of humanists that scientists have not yet come to share.
(C) Controlled measures of aesthetic experience are of little use in the study of the humanities.
(D) Humanists have profited from using methods generally considered useful primarily to scientists.
(E) Fruitful collaboration between scientists and humanists is unlikely to become more common.

GO ON TO THE NEXT PAGE.

9. According to the author, which one of the following is the primary cause of the existing separation between science and the humanities?

    (A) inflammatory claims by scientists regarding the pragmatic value of the work of humanists
    (B) misunderstandings of the philosophical foundations of each by the other
    (C) the excessive influence of reductionism on both
    (D) the predominance of a concern with mechanics in science
    (E) the failure of humanists to develop rigorous methods

10. Which one of the following best describes one of the functions of the last paragraph in the passage?

    (A) to show that a proposal introduced in the first paragraph is implausible because of information presented in the second and third paragraphs
    (B) to show that the views presented in the second and third paragraphs are correct but capable of reconciliation
    (C) to present information supporting one of two opposing views presented in the second and third paragraphs
    (D) to present an alternative to views presented in the second and third paragraphs
    (E) to offer specific examples of the distinct views presented in the second and third paragraphs

11. The passage suggests that the author would recommend that humanists accept which one of the following modifications of their point of view?

    (A) a realization that the scientist is less interested in describing "bodies in motion" than in constructing mathematical models of the material world
    (B) an acknowledgement that there is a spiritual element in the arts that science does not account for
    (C) an acceptance of the application of controlled evaluation to the examination of human values
    (D) a less strident insistence on the primary importance of the arts in people's lives
    (E) an emphasis on developing ways for showing how the humanities support the practical survival of mankind

12. In using the phrase "vagrant fancies of an undisciplined mind" (lines 27–28), the author suggests that humanists are sometimes considered to be

    (A) wildly emotional
    (B) excessively impractical
    (C) unnecessarily intransigent
    (D) justifiably optimistic
    (E) logically inconsistent

GO ON TO THE NEXT PAGE.

The following passages are adapted from critical essays on the American writer Willa Cather (1873–1947).

Passage A

When Cather gave examples of high quality in fiction, she invariably cited Russian writers Ivan Turgenev or Leo Tolstoy or both. Indeed, Edmund Wilson noted in 1922 that Cather followed
(5) the manner of Turgenev, not depicting her characters' emotions directly but telling us how they behave and letting their "inner blaze of glory shine through the simple recital." Turgenev's method was to select details that described a character's appearance and
(10) actions without trying to explain them. A writer, he said, "must be a psychologist—but a secret one; he must know and feel the roots of phenomena, but only present the phenomena themselves." Similarly, he argued that a writer must have complete knowledge
(15) of a character so as to avoid overloading the work with unnecessary detail, concentrating instead on what is characteristic and typical.

Here we have an impressionistic aesthetic that anticipates Cather's: what Turgenev referred to as
(20) secret knowledge Cather called "the thing not named." In one essay she writes that "whatever is felt upon the page without being specifically named there—that, one might say, is created." For both writers, there is the absolute importance of selection and simplification;
(25) for both, art is the fusing of the physical world of setting and actions with the emotional reality of the characters. What synthesizes all the elements of narrative for these writers is the establishment of a prevailing mood.

Passage B

(30) In a famous 1927 letter, Cather writes of her novel *Death Comes for the Archbishop*, "Many [reviewers] assert vehemently that it is not a novel. Myself, I prefer to call it a narrative." Cather's preference anticipated an important reformulation of
(35) the criticism of fiction: the body of literary theory, called "narratology," articulated by French literary theorists in the 1960s. This approach broadens and simplifies the fundamental paradigms according to which we view fiction: they ask of narrative only that
(40) it be narrative, that it tell a story. Narratologists tend *not* to focus on the characteristics of narrative's dominant modern Western form, the "realistic novel": direct psychological characterization, realistic treatment of time, causal plotting, logical closure.
(45) Such a model of criticism, which takes as its object "narrative" rather than the "novel," seems exactly appropriate to Cather's work.

Indeed, her severest critics have always questioned precisely her capabilities as a *novelist*. Morton Zabel
(50) argued that "[Cather's] themes...could readily fail to find the structure and substance that might have given them life or redeemed them from the tenuity of a sketch"; Leon Edel called one of her novels "two inconclusive fragments." These critics and others like
(55) them treat as failures some of the central features of

Cather's impressionistic technique: unusual treatment of narrative time, unexpected focus, ambiguous conclusions, a preference for the bold, simple, and stylized in character as well as in landscape. These
(60) "non-novelistic" structures indirectly articulate the essential and conflicting forces of desire at work throughout Cather's fiction.

13. If the author of passage A were to read passage B, he or she would be most likely to agree with which one of the following?

(A) Though Cather preferred to call *Death Comes for the Archbishop* a narrative rather than a novel, she would be unlikely to view most of her other novels in the same way.

(B) The critics who questioned Cather's abilities as a novelist focused mostly on her failed experiments and ignored her more aesthetically successful novels.

(C) A model of criticism that takes narrative rather than the novel as its object is likely to result in flawed interpretations of Cather's work.

(D) Critics who questioned Cather's abilities as a novelist fail to perceive the extent to which Cather actually embraced the conventions of the realistic novel.

(E) Cather's goal of representing the "thing not named" explains her preference for the bold, simple, and stylized in the presentation of character.

14. Passage B indicates which one of the following?

(A) Narratologists point to Cather's works as prime examples of pure narrative.

(B) Cather disliked the work of many of the novelists who preceded her.

(C) Cather regarded at least one of her works as not fitting straightforwardly into the category of the novel.

(D) Cather's unusual treatment of narrative time was influenced by the Russian writers Turgenev and Tolstoy.

(E) Cather's work was regarded as flawed by most contemporary critics.

GO ON TO THE NEXT PAGE.

15. It can be inferred that both authors would be most likely to regard which one of the following as exemplifying Cather's narrative technique?

(A) A meticulous inventory of the elegant furniture and décor in a character's living room is used to indicate that the character is wealthy.

(B) An account of a character's emotional scars is used to explain the negative effects the character has on his family.

(C) A description of a slightly quivering drink in the hand of a character at a dinner party is used to suggest that the character is timid.

(D) A chronological summary of the events that spark a family conflict is used to supply the context for an in-depth narration of that conflict.

(E) A detailed narration of an unprovoked act of violence and the reprisals it triggers is used to portray the theme that violence begets violence.

16. Which one of the following most accurately states the main point of passage B?

(A) Cather's fiction is best approached by focusing purely on narrative, rather than on the formal characteristics of the novel.

(B) Most commentators on Cather's novels have mistakenly treated her distinctive narrative techniques as aesthetic flaws.

(C) Cather intentionally avoided the realistic psychological characterization that is the central feature of the modern Western novel.

(D) Cather's impressionistic narratives served as an important impetus for the development of narratology in the 1960s.

(E) Cather rejected the narrative constraints of the realistic novel and instead concentrated on portraying her characters by sketching their inner lives.

17. It is most likely that the authors of the two passages would both agree with which one of the following statements?

(A) More than her contemporaries, Cather used stream-of-consciousness narration to portray her characters.

(B) Cather's works were not intended as novels, but rather as narratives.

(C) Narratology is the most appropriate critical approach to Cather's work.

(D) Cather's technique of evoking the "thing not named" had a marked influence on later novelists.

(E) Cather used impressionistic narrative techniques to portray the psychology of her characters.

18. Both authors would be likely to agree that which one of the following, though typical of many novels, would NOT be found in Cather's work?

(A) Description of the salient features of the setting, such as a chair in which a character often sits.

(B) A plot that does not follow chronological time, but rather moves frequently between the novel's past and present.

(C) Description of a character's physical appearance, dress, and facial expressions.

(D) Direct representation of dialogue between the novel's characters, using quotation marks to set off characters' words.

(E) A narration of a character's inner thoughts, including an account of the character's anxieties and wishes.

19. A central purpose of each passage is to

(A) describe the primary influences on Cather's work

(B) identify some of the distinctive characteristics of Cather's work

(C) explain the critical reception Cather's work received in her lifetime

(D) compare Cather's novels to the archetypal form of the realistic novel

(E) examine the impact of European literature and literary theory on Cather's work

GO ON TO THE NEXT PAGE.

Fractal geometry is a mathematical theory devoted to the study of complex shapes called fractals. Although an exact definition of fractals has not been established, fractals commonly exhibit the property of self-similarity:
(5) the reiteration of irregular details or patterns at progressively smaller scales so that each part, when magnified, looks basically like the object as a whole. The Koch curve is a significant fractal in mathematics and examining it provides some insight into fractal
(10) geometry. To generate the Koch curve, one begins with a straight line. The middle third of the line is removed and replaced with two line segments, each as long as the removed piece, which are positioned so as to meet and form the top of a triangle. At this stage,
(15) the curve consists of four connected segments of equal length that form a pointed protrusion in the middle. This process is repeated on the four segments so that all the protrusions are on the same side of the curve, and then the process is repeated indefinitely on the
(20) segments at each stage of the construction.

Self-similarity is built into the construction process by treating segments at each stage the same way as the original segment was treated. Since the rules for getting from one stage to another are fully
(25) explicit and always the same, images of successive stages of the process can be generated by computer. Theoretically, the Koch curve is the result of infinitely many steps in the construction process, but the finest image approximating the Koch curve will be limited
(30) by the fact that eventually the segments will get too short to be drawn or displayed. However, using computer graphics to produce images of successive stages of the construction process dramatically illustrates a major attraction of fractal geometry:
(35) simple processes can be responsible for incredibly complex patterns.

A worldwide public has become captivated by fractal geometry after viewing astonishing computer-generated images of fractals; enthusiastic practitioners
(40) in the field of fractal geometry consider it a new language for describing complex natural and mathematical forms. They anticipate that fractal geometry's significance will rival that of calculus and expect that proficiency in fractal geometry will allow
(45) mathematicians to describe the form of a cloud as easily and precisely as an architect can describe a house using the language of traditional geometry. Other mathematicians have reservations about the fractal geometers' preoccupation with computer-generated
(50) graphic images and their lack of interest in theory. These mathematicians point out that traditional mathematics consists of proving theorems, and while many theorems about fractals have already been proven using the notions of pre-fractal mathematics,
(55) fractal geometers have proven only a handful of theorems that could not have been proven with pre-fractal mathematics. According to these mathematicians, fractal geometry can attain a lasting role in mathematics only if it becomes a precise
(60) language supporting a system of theorems and proofs.

20. Which one of the following most accurately expresses the main point of the passage?

(A) Because of its unique forms, fractal geometry is especially adaptable to computer technology and is therefore likely to grow in importance and render pre-fractal mathematics obsolete.

(B) Though its use in the generation of extremely complex forms makes fractal geometry an intriguing new mathematical theory, it is not yet universally regarded as having attained the theoretical rigor of traditional mathematics.

(C) Fractal geometry is significant because of its use of self-similarity, a concept that has enabled geometers to generate extremely detailed computer images of natural forms.

(D) Using the Koch curve as a model, fractal geometers have developed a new mathematical language that is especially useful in technological contexts because it does not rely on theorems.

(E) Though fractal geometry has thus far been of great value for its capacity to define abstract mathematical shapes, it is not expected to be useful for the description of ordinary natural shapes.

21. Which one of the following is closest to the meaning of the phrase "fully explicit" as used in lines 24–25?

(A) illustrated by an example
(B) uncomplicated
(C) expressed unambiguously
(D) in need of lengthy computation
(E) agreed on by all

22. According to the description in the passage, each one of the following illustrates the concept of self-similarity EXCEPT:

(A) Any branch broken off a tree looks like the tree itself.
(B) Each portion of the intricately patterned frost on a window looks like the pattern as a whole.
(C) The pattern of blood vessels in each part of the human body is similar to the pattern of blood vessels in the entire body.
(D) The seeds of several subspecies of maple tree resemble one another in shape despite differences in size.
(E) The florets composing a cauliflower head resemble the entire cauliflower head.

GO ON TO THE NEXT PAGE.

23. The explanation of how a Koch curve is generated (lines 10–20) serves primarily to

 (A) show how fractal geometry can be reduced to traditional geometry
 (B) give an example of a natural form that can be described by fractal geometry
 (C) anticipate the objection that fractal geometry is not a precise language
 (D) illustrate the concept of self-similarity
 (E) provide an exact definition of fractals

24. Which one of the following does the author present as a characteristic of fractal geometry?

 (A) It is potentially much more important than calculus.
 (B) Its role in traditional mathematics will expand as computers become faster.
 (C) It is the fastest-growing field of mathematics.
 (D) It encourages the use of computer programs to prove mathematical theorems.
 (E) It enables geometers to generate complex forms using simple processes.

25. Each of the following statements about the Koch curve can be properly deduced from the information given in the passage EXCEPT:

 (A) The total number of protrusions in the Koch curve at any stage of the construction depends on the length of the initial line chosen for the construction.
 (B) The line segments at each successive stage of the construction of the Koch curve are shorter than the segments at the previous stage.
 (C) Theoretically, as the Koch curve is constructed its line segments become infinitely small.
 (D) At every stage of constructing the Koch curve, all the line segments composing it are of equal length.
 (E) The length of the line segments in the Koch curve at any stage of its construction depends on the length of the initial line chosen for the construction.

26. The enthusiastic practitioners of fractal geometry mentioned in lines 39–40 would be most likely to agree with which one of the following statements?

 (A) The Koch curve is the most easily generated, and therefore the most important, of the forms studied by fractal geometers.
 (B) Fractal geometry will eventually be able to be used in the same applications for which traditional geometry is now used.
 (C) The greatest importance of computer images of fractals is their ability to bring fractal geometry to the attention of a wider public.
 (D) Studying self-similarity was impossible before the development of sophisticated computer technologies.
 (E) Certain complex natural forms exhibit a type of self-similarity like that exhibited by fractals.

27. The information in the passage best supports which one of the following assertions?

 (A) The appeal of a mathematical theory is limited to those individuals who can grasp the theorems and proofs produced in that theory.
 (B) Most of the important recent breakthroughs in mathematical theory would not have been possible without the ability of computers to graphically represent complex shapes.
 (C) Fractal geometry holds the potential to replace traditional geometry in most of its engineering applications.
 (D) A mathematical theory can be developed and find applications even before it establishes a precise definition of its subject matter.
 (E) Only a mathematical theory that supports a system of theorems and proofs will gain enthusiastic support among a significant number of mathematicians.

S T O P

IF YOU FINISH BEFORE TIME IS CALLED, YOU MAY CHECK YOUR WORK ON THIS SECTION ONLY.
DO NOT WORK ON ANY OTHER SECTION IN THE TEST.

Acknowledgment is made to the following sources from which material has been adapted for use in this test booklet:

Jerome Barron, *Freedom of the Press for Whom? The Right of Access to Mass Media.* ©1973 by Indiana University Press.

Huw Jones, "Fractals Before Mandelbrot: A Selective History." ©1993 by Springer-Verlag New York Inc.

Wait for the supervisor's instructions before you open the page to the topic.
Please print and sign your name and write the date in the designated spaces below.

Time: 35 Minutes

General Directions

You will have 35 minutes in which to plan and write an essay on the topic inside. Read the topic and the accompanying directions carefully. You will probably find it best to spend a few minutes considering the topic and organizing your thoughts before you begin writing. In your essay, be sure to develop your ideas fully, leaving time, if possible, to review what you have written. **Do not write on a topic other than the one specified. Writing on a topic of your own choice is not acceptable.**

No special knowledge is required or expected for this writing exercise. Law schools are interested in the reasoning, clarity, organization, language usage, and writing mechanics displayed in your essay. How well you write is more important than how much you write.

Confine your essay to the blocked, lined area on the front and back of the separate Writing Sample Response Sheet. Only that area will be reproduced for law schools. Be sure that your writing is legible.

Both this topic sheet and your response sheet must be turned over to the testing staff before you leave the room.

Topic Code	Print Your Full Name Here		
080102	Last	First	M.I.
Date	Sign Your Name Here		
/ /			

Scratch Paper
Do not write your essay in this space.

LSAT® Writing Sample Topic

<u>Directions</u>: The scenario presented below describes two choices, either one of which can be supported on the basis of the information given. Your essay should consider both choices and argue for one over the other, based on the two specified criteria and the facts provided. There is no "right" or "wrong" choice: a reasonable argument can be made for either.

Linda intends to spend her vacation walking part of a national trail. Over the course of one week, she will walk the trail while her luggage is taken on ahead of her each day. At this point, she must choose between either making all the arrangements herself or hiring a company that organizes walking tours to do this for her. Using the facts below, write an essay in which you argue for one approach over the other, based on the following two criteria:

- Linda wants to minimize the effort she puts into managing the vacation, both prior to and during the walk.
- She wants to have as much control over each day's experience as possible.

If Linda chooses to design her own walk and make the arrangements herself, she will research the trail and the available accommodations to estimate the distance she can comfortably cover each day and determine appropriate nightly stopover points. She will arrange for the luggage transportation and lodging. During her walk, it will be easy for her to add rest days as needed and otherwise change her itinerary from day to day.

If she hires a company that organizes walking tours, the company will plan the length of each day's walk based on its knowledge of the terrain. Linda will designate any planned rest days ahead of time. The walking company typically chooses among a limited set of nightly accommodations that it has selected based on customer feedback, honoring specific requests when possible. She will walk on her own. Complete lodging and route details will be provided to her the evening before her first day out. The company will oversee day-to-day luggage transportation.

WP-Q080A

Scratch Paper
Do not write your essay in this space.

LAST NAME (Print)

L

FIRST NAME (Print)

SSN/ SIN

MI

TEST CENTER NO.

SIGNATURE

M M D D Y Y

TEST DATE

LSAC ACCOUNT NO.

TOPIC CODE

Writing Sample Response Sheet

DO NOT WRITE IN THIS SPACE

Begin your essay in the lined area below.
Continue on the back if you need more space.

Directions:

1. Use the Answer Key on the next page to check your answers.

2. Use the Scoring Worksheet below to compute your raw score.

3. Use the Score Conversion Chart to convert your raw score into the 120-180 scale.

Scoring Worksheet

1. Enter the number of questions you answered correctly in each section.

	Number Correct
SECTION I	_____
SECTION II	_____
SECTION III	_____
SECTION IV	_____

2. Enter the sum here: _____
   This is your Raw Score.

Conversion Chart

For Converting Raw Score to the 120-180 LSAT Scaled Score
LSAT Form 0LSN87

Reported Score	Raw Score Lowest	Raw Score Highest
180	99	101
179	98	98
178	—*	—*
177	97	97
176	96	96
175	95	95
174	94	94
173	93	93
172	92	92
171	91	91
170	90	90
169	89	89
168	87	88
167	86	86
166	84	85
165	83	83
164	81	82
163	80	80
162	78	79
161	76	77
160	75	75
159	73	74
158	71	72
157	69	70
156	68	68
155	66	67
154	64	65
153	62	63
152	61	61
151	59	60
150	57	58
149	55	56
148	54	54
147	52	53
146	50	51
145	49	49
144	47	48
143	45	46
142	44	44
141	42	43
140	41	41
139	39	40
138	37	38
137	36	36
136	34	35
135	33	33
134	32	32
133	30	31
132	29	29
131	27	28
130	26	26
129	25	25
128	23	24
127	22	22
126	21	21
125	20	20
124	18	19
123	17	17
122	15	16
121	—*	—*
120	0	14

*There is no raw score that will produce this scaled score for this form.

SECTION I

1.	D	8.	E	15.	E	22.	D
2.	B	9.	D	16.	A	23.	E
3.	C	10.	C	17.	B		
4.	D	11.	B	18.	C		
5.	C	12.	B	19.	D		
6.	B	13.	D	20.	E		
7.	B	14.	A	21.	B		

SECTION II

1.	A	8.	E	15.	A	22.	A
2.	A	9.	C	16.	B	23.	B
3.	D	10.	B	17.	E	24.	E
4.	D	11.	C	18.	D	25.	C
5.	E	12.	D	19.	C	26.	B
6.	C	13.	C	20.	D		
7.	A	14.	E	21.	E		

SECTION III

1.	A	8.	C	15.	C	22.	B
2.	C	9.	D	16.	C	23.	C
3.	A	10.	C	17.	D	24.	C
4.	B	11.	A	18.	B	25.	E
5.	A	12.	E	19.	D		
6.	A	13.	D	20.	E		
7.	C	14.	D	21.	B		

SECTION IV

1.	A	8.	D	15.	C	22.	D
2.	A	9.	B	16.	A	23.	D
3.	D	10.	D	17.	E	24.	E
4.	C	11.	C	18.	E	25.	A
5.	E	12.	B	19.	B	26.	E
6.	E	13.	E	20.	B	27.	D
7.	C	14.	C	21.	C		

LSAT® Prep Tools

LSAT ItemWise®

Get to know the LSAT

LSAC's popular, online LSAT familiarization tool, *LSAT ItemWise*:

- includes all three types of LSAT questions—logical reasoning, analytical reasoning, and reading comprehension;

- keeps track of your answers; and

- shows you explanations as to why answers are correct or incorrect.

Although it is best to use our paper-and-pencil *Official LSAT PrepTest®* products to fully prepare for the LSAT, you can enhance your preparation by understanding all three question types and why your answers are right or wrong.

ItemWise includes an introduction to the new reading comprehension question type—comparative reading—with sample questions and explanations.

LSAC account holders get unlimited online access to *ItemWise* for the length of the account.

$18